MEN OF

By the same author:

Gadfly for God (Hodder & Stoughton 1991)
High and Mitred (SPCK 1992)
Reverend Rebels (DLT 1993)

MEN OF HABIT

The Franciscan Ideal in Action

BERNARD PALMER

Foreword by
The Archbishop of Canterbury

The Canterbury Press
Norwich

To the members of
THE SOCIETY OF ST FRANCIS
who provided me with the
inspiration for this book.

© Bernard Palmer 1994

First published 1994 by The Canterbury Press Norwich
(a publishing imprint of Hymns Ancient & Modern Limited,
a registered charity)
St Mary's Works, St Mary's Plain,
Norwich, Norfolk, NR3 3BH

British Library Cataloguing in Publication Data

A catalogue record for this book is available
from the British Library

ISBN 1–85311–092–2

Typeset by Datix International Limited
Bungay, Suffolk and
Printed and bound in Great Britain by
St Edmundsbury Press Limited
Bury St Edmunds, Suffolk

FOREWORD

*By the Most Revd and Rt Hon. George Carey
the Lord Archbishop of Canterbury*

I have said on several occasions that the Church of England's religious communities are among its richest treasures – and its best kept secrets! From these communities have come many remarkable people of vision, faith and bold commitment, whose contribution to the life and health of our Church is incalculable.

In this book Bernard Palmer describes four such men – Father Andrew, Brother Douglas, George Potter and Brother Edward. All four were people who epitomised the Franciscan ideal of evangelical simplicity and catholic faith; each one embodied the incarnational spirit of monasticism and each one radiated the love of God. As they come to life in these pages it is heartening to see that they were also people who knew the difficulties of facing doubt and fear. It is encouraging too to see them discovering God's will for their lives, in the midst of their struggles.

In an age when people are beguiled by the belief that what matters in life is to achieve material prosperity, success and fame, it is good to remember what God can do when we hand over our lives to him. *Men of Habit* reminds us that 'giving up' is never a negative act in the Christian pilgrimage, but is rather a getaway to new life itself.

George Carey

CONTENTS

PREFACE

ON MIGRATING FROM KENT to Dorset in late 1989
after retiring from the editorship of the *Church Times* I discovered
that my new home was only ten miles from the headquarters of
the Society of St Francis at Hilfield, near Cerne Abbas – an hour
or so away by push-bike along delightful lanes. So, when I was
looking around me in 1993 for a subject for a new book, my
thoughts turned naturally to the Franciscans – and, more particularly, to Brother Douglas. As a teenager I had heard him preach
on several occasions; and his sermons, or more probably the
preacher himself, had left a strong impression on my mind. A
year or two before his death I met him face to face for the first
time, when he agreed to be interviewed for an article in the
Church Times: I was then deeply moved by the charm of his
personality. However, when it came to writing about him forty
years later, there seemed little point in attempting a full-scale
biography, which could be little more than a paraphrase of Fr
Francis's life of 1959. So I decided instead to include him in a
series of mini-biographies of four notable religious who were
near-contemporaries and had all flourished in the first half of
this century – the others being Fr Andrew, SDC; Fr George
Potter, BHC; and Brother Edward, of the Village Evangelists.
All four men were examplars of the Franciscan ideal in action.
The first three founded, or helped to found, religious communities or organizations and were the guiding lights of those

communities in their formative years. But, in two cases out of three, the communities failed to survive their founders by more than a few years; and, in the third case, the SSF only survived because the unsystematic outreach of Brother Douglas was balanced by the organizational ability of Fr Algy. Thus the connecting link between my first three 'lives' is to show that charisma by itself is not enough, and that communities kept going by the personal example and inspiration of a single individual are unlikely to survive once that individual's influence has been removed by death.

My fourth subject, Brother Edward, was not a 'religious' in the strictly technical sense, except for the few months that he was a postulant and then a novice at Cowley; but, in his patched and faded cassock, he was very much a 'man of habit' and therefore, I feel, justifies his inclusion in the book. His life was certainly lived in the spirit of St Francis, even though his unwillingness to take the vow of obedience, and indeed his unorthodox views on how a community ought to be constituted, meant that he could never be a member of a traditional religious order – even the Society of St Francis, with which he had so much in common. But, with his personal charisma, he was certainly on a par with my other three protagonists.

BERNARD PALMER
Charminister, Dorset
March 1994

ACKNOWLEDGEMENTS

MY GRATITUDE IS DUE, first and foremost, to the members of the Society of St Francis for their assistance and encouragement in enabling me to carry out the necessary research for this book both at Hilfield and at the Bodleian, and for their general goodwill towards the project. In particular I should like to thank Brother Sam, the Guardian at Hilfield; Brother Reginald, the Archivist; Brother Martin, the Provincial Secretary; and Brother Edward, of Plaistow. All four were especially kind and helpful in responding to my various requests. I must also thank the authorities of the Bodleian Library at Oxford for kindly allowing me access to the SSF Deposit.

A work such as this is bound to draw heavily on existing biographies. I should like here to acknowledge my particular debt to A. R. Mowbray & Co. for permission to quote from Kathleen E. Burne's *The Life and Letters of Father Andrew*, SDC., Father Francis's *Brother Douglas: Apostle of the Outcast* and *Tales of Brother Douglas*, by George Seaver & Coleman Jennings; to Harper Collins for permission to quote from Kenneth Packard's *Brother Edward: Priest and Evangelist*; and to Hodder & Stoughton for permission to quote from George Potter's *Father Potter of Peckham* and *More Father Potter of Peckham*. I am also immensely grateful to Mrs Joanna Kelley both for allowing me free access to the Brother Edward archive in her London home and for granting me permission to photocopy and quote freely from her own unpublished memoir of Edward. Among more general books, Barrie Williams's *The Franciscan Revival in the Anglican Communion* has proved a mine of useful information.

I must express my gratitude to all those readers of the *Church Times*, too numerous to mention individually, who so kindly responded to my published request in the paper for information concerning my four major characters. I am also indebted to Bishop Leslie Lloyd Rees for his recollections of George Potter as a prison visitor; to Mrs Margaret Duggan for presenting me with a copy of her booklet, *The Convent of the Sisters of the Community of Jesus of Nazareth, Westcote*; to Mr Steven Saxby for making me a copy of a tape-recording of memories of Fr Andrew; and to Mr David Stewart for supplying me with copies of the birth certificates of both Brother Douglas and Fr George, together with information (derived from census returns) concerning the members of their families.

Last but not least, I thank my wife for once again converting my messy typescript into an impeccable fair copy for the publishers, and for helpful criticisms and much-needed encouragement.

B.P.

FRANCISCAN PIONEER

Claude Harris

Fr Andrew, SDC, in his forties.

CHAPTER 1

FRANCISCAN PIONEER

*Fr Andrew and the Society of the Divine
Compassion*

AN AGNOSTIC SCHOOLBOY, curious to know why his
mother thought it worth while to travel so far to church each
week in order to listen to a certain Fr Andrew, asked to
accompany her one Sunday. Afterwards he said to her: 'Mother,
that was the most terrifying service I ever was at. It made me
sweat all over'. On being asked *why*, he replied: 'It was the first
service I ever went to at which I felt something *really happened*'.
What manner of man was it who could evoke such an unlikely
response from a cynical teenager? The answer, in a nutshell, was
a man who radiated holiness. As his close friend Lucy Menzies
put it: 'He somehow took us up into the supernatural'. This
sense of being transported into another world was especially
apparent when he celebrated the Eucharist. A missionary home
on leave remarked with awe: 'I have seen priests celebrate the
Mass practically all over the world, but never one who celebrated
as this old priest does'. A young widow whose husband, a pilot
in the RAF, had been shot down during the Second World War
and who had been comforted in her bereavement by Fr Andrew,
penned a moving tribute to him: 'It isn't only what he says or
writes or teaches, but essentially what he *is*. When one is with
him one just doesn't *have* any problems. There doesn't seem to
be anything worth worrying about. He carries about with him
too much of the peace of God'. Bishop Buxton of Gibraltar
summed it all up when he remarked a year after his death: 'He

was a great man, such as God sends us only one or two in a generation'. And not the least part of his greatness, at any rate in the context of this book, was the role he played in restoring an active Franciscanism to the life and witness of the Church of England.

*   *   *

The man who was to become Fr Andrew in religion began life as Henry Ernest Hardy. He was born at Kasauli, India, on 7 January 1869, the fourth son of Colonel Edmund Armitage Hardy and Grace Maxwell Aiken. His father, a man of great personal courage and integrity, had served all through the Indian Mutiny. During one engagement he had had three horses shot under him; during another he had fought all night with a bullet in his leg. At the start of the Mutiny he had been in command of a Sepoy regiment; but his men had refused to join the rebels because he had always respected their religious scruples and never asked them to do things to which their consciences were opposed. Ernest's mother, also a person of character, was a descendant of Susannah, the sister of Nicholas Ferrar of Little Gidding, the greatest mystic in the Church of England of his day. Both his parents were fervent Evangelicals of exemplary piety and devotion. Ernest once recalled waking as a small boy in the night and hearing his father praying aloud, his voice 'shaking with emotion . . . he was praying for each one of us; he was praying for me'. There was another side, of course, to the Evangelical coin. When Ernest decided to join a religious community it was a great disappointment to his parents, who had no understanding of or sympathy with Catholic teaching and would have preferred him to go into the parochial ministry. To the colonel Ernest's monkish habit was at first an offensive eccentricity, though after a time he relented and father and son resumed their former affectionate relationship.

Ernest spent his childhood in India – and it began with one terrifying episode which he loved to relate. His mother was journeying through the jungle with the new-born Ernest to rejoin his father after her confinement. She was accompanied by eight native bearers, but the trip was still full of hazards. One particular night she spent in a dhak bungalow by the side of the jungle track. After supper she settled down to read a book by the light of her lamp. The french windows were wide open. What followed can best be told in Ernest's own words:

> My mother, tired with the day's journey, was mentally far away, thinking long thoughts and wholly unconscious of any danger, when she was in an instant recalled to intensest activity and concentration on the present moment by a low growl; and there, already in the room, was a great panther who had come in from the jungle through the open window, no doubt scenting the food on the table, and was now bent on having a new English baby for his evening repast. My mother rose in a moment, took the lamp from the table, went up to the creature, and thrust the lamp in its face. Mercifully it whipped round and leapt out lightly into the jungle again, this time carrying off with it a poor kid that was tethered in the compound round the bungalow.

The moment of shared peril may well have set up a psychological bond between mother and son. Certainly there was an exceptionally close tie between them. As a child Ernest almost worshipped his mother, and to the end of his life he carried a miniature of her in his dispatch-case which he delighted to show to anyone who he thought might be interested. In a letter written in 1945, less than a year before his death, he describes her as an Evangelical saint. 'I remember so well that once I had been preaching about the Blessed Sacrament when she was present in the congregation. When I got into the carriage to drive home with her she threw her arms round me and said: "You know, dear, you said what I have always believed, but I never knew how to express it."'

When Colonel Hardy retired from the Army the family settled at Clifton, on the outskirts of Bristol. A childhood friend remembered the Ernest of those days as a rather plain little boy with a big nose and bright red hair. But his parents' piety must already have made its mark on his young mind because the same friend also recalled that there were somehow fewer quarrels among the neighbouring children when Ernest was present. As a child, however, he was delicate. He went to school for a short

while at Clifton College, but then persuaded his parents to
withdraw him and send him instead to an art school in Bristol.
He had long had a passion for drawing and painting, and could
now indulge his hobby to the full with a view to making it his
career. The Almighty, however, had other plans for him. He
stayed two years at the school, spending his afternoons painting
in the Leigh Woods beyond the river Avon and his evenings in
drawing from life. But then his eldest sister Constance, duty-
loving but primly censorious, accused him of idling away his
time. 'Ernest', she is reported to have said, 'you are deteriorat-
ing!' He took the hint and told his father that he would like to
give up art and go to Oxford instead. After a period of cramming
to restore his lost Latin and Greek he joined his eldest brother
Frank at Keble College in October 1888 and appeared to enjoy
the easygoing life of a typical undergraduate. Indeed his biographer, Kathleen Burne, likens his activities at this period to those
of the saint whose example he was soon to follow. 'There is a
very real parallel . . . Like St Francis he grew up in comfortable
circumstances and enjoyed the gay and easy companionship of
his fellows: care-free and popular, he had an intense appreciation
of all the good things and pleasures of life.' He wrote weekly
letters to his mother embellished with amusing pen-and-ink
drawings – which generally included one of his dog: 'my usual
trade-mark, without which nothing is genuine'. His love of dogs
continued to the end of his life.

What was his attitude to religion at this time? He had been
confirmed while a schoolboy at Clifton, though in after-years he
reflected that the instruction given by his headmaster, Canon
J.M. Wilson, had not left much of an impression. 'And yet, for
all the unreality that marked my life then, I can remember as one
of the most vital and real experiences of my life the actual
moment of my confirmation. I can never forget the feeling that
the hand of God had been laid on me, and that something
intensely real beyond all the make-believe business had really
happened . . . I remember the sacramental sense of contact with
the supernatural presence of God.' At Oxford the impetus was
absent. As he described it (in the third person) many years later,
his motive in forsaking art for the study of theology had been

'to get a theory to live by and a quest to follow'. However, 'entirely through his own fault the result was a heavy disappointment. He found in the history of the Church no great romance, nor did he discover in the representatives of the priesthood or the society of professing Churchmen the satisfaction of his discontent'. Ernest passed his Oxford days without any set religious convictions or real understanding of religion. Although thinking vaguely in terms of ordination, his attitude to it at this stage was no more than luke-warm. His prospects were hardly helped by his modest academic achievements. He could manage no more than a fourth-class degree in theology – though his poor showing was due more to health problems (hay-fever and eye-trouble) than to deliberate idleness.

The man who was to revolutionize his attitude towards religion was the future Bishop of London, A.F. Winnington-Ingram, then head of the Oxford House at Bethnal Green, whom Ernest had met during his last year at the university. Oxford House was intended as a place where university men could serve the underprivileged. In its early days it exuded an air of patronage. Scott Holland dismissed it as a 'home for the rich unemployed' wherein 'submerged gentlemen' could take shelter and be brought under the 'healthy influence of contact with the working man. They gain the hope and vigour that comes from real usefulness'. Or, as Ernest himself put it long afterwards, Winnington-Ingram was appealing for volunteers to 'live the life of the ordinary English gentleman, but to live it in the East instead of the West End of London'. However, Ernest was thrilled at the immediate prospect and was able to report enthusiastically to his mother on 25 February 1890 regarding the fateful meeting that was to divert his life into more fruitful channels:

> An awfully nice parson came down here the other day, Ingram of Oxford House, Bethnal Green. He held a meeting without being a bit parsonish, and I like him awfully . . . I think that, if Pater will let me, I should like to go up to Bethnal Green for some time, a year if possible, after I have taken my degree. It would be three times as good as going to a Theological College where they have

nothing but smug prayers all day ... What chiefly struck me
about Ingram was that he was such an awfully happy chap and so
absolutely free from any sort of cant.

Ernest refrained from telling his mother that it was his fear of
being left alone with a clergyman that had led him to invite a
friend to join himself and Ingram over tea!

Ingram was keen for Ernest to come and help him; and
accordingly, in October 1891, he took up residence at Oxford
House. His duties combined administration with practical welfare work. He had to keep notes of the cases that needed visiting
and to see to the organization's accounts, as well as being one of
the actual visitors, teaching in the clubs for men and boys and
generally playing a prominent part in the multifarious activities
going on. He soon found himself in his element. 'I never was so
happy in my life before', he wrote to his father soon after his
arrival, 'and work like a lark from morning to night'. But he
regarded his spell of duty as no more than temporary and was
now thinking much more enthusiastically about the prospect of
ordination. In July 1892 he told his father that Ely would be his
preferred theological college, 'as they don't let you smoke and
they make you sit up generally; and I think that, preparing for a
great step like the taking of Holy Orders, one needs a good
stern discipline to start with'. He added that, once ordained, he
wanted to go to a slum – 'and should like to stay in a slum all
my life'.

Oxford House undoubtedly supplied Ernest with much of the
motivation to go forward to ordination. But it was not the
whole story. Shortly after his arrival there an incident occurred
which he regarded as the second turning-point of his career, his
crucial meeting with Ingram being the first. He described the
incident in his book, *The Adventure of Faith* – and dogs played a
critical part in it.

The story began when, shortly before he was due to start
work at Bethnal Green, his father told him of how, when in
command of a cavalry regiment in India, he had been bitten in
the leg by a dog believed to be suffering from hydrophobia.
Terrified of falling victim to the disease and alone at the time,

the colonel had cauterized with a hot iron the place on his leg where he had been bitten – and still bore the scar. The day after hearing this tale from his father Ernest visited a friend who ran a dogs' home in Bristol – and was himself bitten by one of its inmates. A chemist treated the bite with caustic soda and a doctor told him to hope for the best; but it was with the fear of hydrophobia at the back of his mind that Ernest began his spell of duty at Oxford House. The third act in the drama occurred a short while later. One day in the Bethnal Green Road the fear descended on him with such power that he 'felt a sensation of positive physical choking and, crushed by a palpable darkness, literally staggered back to the settlement-house'. He went into the chapel of the house, lay down before the altar and prayed. His prayer ended: 'Father, is my life to be just a passage from darkness into darkness? I have made a mess of my life myself; if you can do anything with it, I will give my life to you, and I will never ask it back again'. Ernest then says that he passed into a state of unconsciousness. When he became conscious again he found himself lying with his head on the altar step – and 'felt much as a baby might who had been asleep for hours and had waked refreshed to be kissed by a very loving mother. The fear was gone and the world seemed a different place, and there was an absolute spiritual certainty that prayer to God in the Name of our Lord Jesus Christ had been an effective thing and that a real spiritual compact with God had been made'.

It was this traumatic experience, beginning with his father's horror story and ending with his own vision of God at the altar in Bethnal Green, that, according to Ernest, first turned his thoughts to the religious life. But it was to be the religious life attached to a particular locality – the East End. As he put it in a letter to his mother: 'I would sooner have one year in Bethnal Green than twenty in Belgravia'. The problem now was to find a way of combining a vocation to the religious life with a parallel vocation to work among the impoverished masses of East London. The answer to the problem came as a result of another fateful meeting: this time with Ingram's predecessor as head of the Oxford House, the Revd and Hon. James Adderley.

*   *   *

James Granville Adderley (1861–1942) was the fifth and youngest son of Sir Charles Bowyer Adderley, a high-minded Christian
statesman who in 1878 was ennobled as the first Baron Norton.
James was educated at Eton and Christ Church, Oxford, where
he was the moving spirit behind the Philothespians, forerunners
of the Oxford University Dramatic Society. Little is known of
his religious life at Oxford, though his biographer thinks that he
was much influenced by the powerful preaching of Henry Scott
Holland. After graduating he worked for a time in a London
solicitor's office. But he was so affected by the social and
spiritual needs of East London that he abandoned the Law and
was appointed the first head of the Oxford House in Bethnal
Green. He stayed there eighteen months, but was then ordained
and served a succession of curacies in East London, ending up
at St Andrew's, Plaistow. It was shortly before his move to
Plaistow that the event occurred that was to cause his name for a
short while to hit the headlines. This was the publication of his
semi-autobiographical novel, *Stephen Remarx*, which, after being
refused by twenty publishers, was eventually accepted, rapidly
became a best-seller and ran to twelve editions. The hero,
nephew of a marquess, shocks his rich friends and relatives by
his Christian Socialist ideals and eventually founds a religious
community where he can put those ideals into practice. The
author rightly claimed that the book had caught the mood of the
times. It was a parable of his own convictions, soon found its
way into the common-room of the Oxford House – and was
eagerly devoured by Ernest Hardy.

It was not therefore surprising that, when Ernest met Adderley shortly after the publication of *Stephen Remarx*, he should
have been at once attracted to a man whose ideals were so
similar to his own. They were joined by a third enthusiast,
Henry Rivington Chappel, a Cornish rector's son who, like the
other two men, hungered for something different from the
menage of the ordinary parsonage or clergy-house. Chappel was
a scholar who had sat at the feet of Charles Gore. He had
recently been ordained and, according to Ernest, was 'a man of

absolutely unblemished life and with no interests apart from the actual concerns of definite religion'. Before long the three men were flirting with the idea of founding a new religious community on the lines of the fictional one adumbrated in *Stephen Remarx*. Adderley claimed later that he had always wanted to be 'a sort of friar'. He had even advertised in the *Church Times* for a like-minded priest to come and live with him. The only reply he had received on that occasion had been one from Walter Howard Frere, the future Superior of the Community of the Resurrection and Bishop of Truro, and nothing had come of the idea. But, with two new associates to egg him on, the time was now much more propitious. Describing the origins of the SDC in an article published in the Anglo-Catholic *Green Quarterly* for April 1924, Ernest wrote: 'The Socialist with his dreams, the scholar with his creed, and the art student with his particular experience, found themselves together . . . asking themselves whence had been the impulse and whither was to be the leading of this beginning of their comradeship'. In January 1894 the three men went on a retreat to Pusey House, Oxford, where their mutual friend Fr Philip Waggett then a novice at Cowley, drew up a rule of life for them. On the morning of 20 January, after Mass had been celebrated, they bound themselves to the rule, and to the three religious vows of poverty, chastity and obedience, for one year. Later in the day Adderley and Chappel went direct to Plaistow to take charge of the mission church and district of St Philip. At that time the district lay in the diocese of St Albans, though in 1914 it became part of the diocese of Chelmsford.

The new community was christened the Society of the Divine Compassion (at the suggestion of Ernest, 'in gratitude to God's amazing goodness in the experience of his own life'). Although its rule and way of life resembled those of the original followers of St Francis of Assisi, its motivation was not specifically Franciscan. According to Peter Anson the SDC came into being, as far as Adderley was concerned, from his conviction that the Co-operative Movement, Trade Unionism and Socialism had all failed, largely because working men were unwilling to accept leadership. 'Hence the hope that the example of a small group of men living under vows of poverty, chastity and obedience might achieve more in the long run than further schemes for social reform.' On the other hand, says Anson, while Adderley's two colleagues shared his social conscience, they were probably more concerned than he was with the religious life as an end in itself. Nevertheless, the SDC 'evolved into a quasi-Franciscan community simply because its ideals were akin to those of St Francis – to imitate literally the life of Christ*. An early recruit, George Tate (who later went over to Rome), observed that, though the spirit of St Francis was the SDC's chief characteristic, it was 'St Francis's spirit in Church of England conditions'. There was no attempt to ape the way of life of Roman Catholic Franciscan houses. The society was defined as 'a community of priests, deacons and communicant laymen banded together in a common life of Poverty, Chastity and Obedience for the glory of our Lord and Saviour Jesus Christ and the benefit of His Holy Catholic Church, to worship Him and to work for Him and all mankind, especially the poor and suffering, in imitation of the Divine Master, seeking the help of one another in thus obeying Him'.

In the meantime, while Adderley and Chappel were busy setting the wheels in motion at Plaistow, Ernest had returned to Ely to complete his training for the sacred ministry. In the regular letters which he wrote to his mother between his arrival in April 1893 and his departure in March 1894 it is possible to trace the development of his plans for the future. At first he enthuses about the peace of his surroundings: 'There is a sort of holy hush about the whole place which is very refreshing after London . . . the very tradesmen look like Minor Canons'. Later, however, he voices his relief at the 'certainty of a life of absolute and continuous activity' that lies before him. 'I don't have the guilty feeling that I am sitting still while others are suffering, as

---

*In a telling comment he made on the origins of the SDC Reginald Tribe wrote: 'This band of men who (like St Francis) have embraced a sanctified poverty and helped to take away the reproach that the Church was not spiritual enough to carry out her Master's precepts and renounce riches and comfort . . . It is very hard for the masses to realise the sincerity of those who, coming to preach to them the brotherhood of man, are probably the only people in the parish who keep a servant'.

I did in my first term.' He was made deacon on Trinity Sunday, 20 May 1894, by Bishop Festing of St Albans, who priested him a year later – the first priest of the Church of England to be ordained in a religious habit since the Reformation. Fr Andrew (Ernest's new name in religion) told his mother how kind everyone had been at his ordination – even the Archdeacon, 'who is quite an old-fashioned clergyman whom I was afraid my habit would annoy'. 'It is a great joy to me', he added, 'that I have never yet had a quarrel with anyone about my religious convictions.'

*   *   *

The new community was built on the twin foundations of faith and works. As Andrew commented on one occasion: 'There will be no rivalry between the two. Prayer will sanctify work; work will give prayer its practical expression. One brother will peel potatoes with the greater tranquillity because another is praying in the chapel'. There was certainly plenty of scope for work. The district of London in which the community was based was one of the poorest in the capital. Unemployment, disease, dirt and drunkenness were rife – and there was often real starvation. In one letter to his mother Andrew tells her that the brothers have been eating dry bread – 'some of them saying that they had no heart to eat anything else with the knowledge of the poverty all round. We get twenty-five men a day, on an average, begging just for a crust of dry bread and ever so thankful to get that'. And in another letter he says that he has found families 'without even the light of a candle sitting silently and starving in the dark'. But of course there was always the subtle distinction between those, like the members of the SDC, who embraced poverty voluntarily and those who had it thrust upon them. As Adderley himself said after a night spent on the London Embankment among the down-and-outs: '*We* can get breakfast and a bath, and the poor can't: that's the difference'. And he enjoyed quoting a remark made by the then Bishop of London, Frederick Temple, against him: 'Shall I tell you why he [Adderley] can never be really poor? Because he washes!' Nevertheless, the living conditions for the members of the community were austere. There was no carpet on the floors and a fire only in the common-room. Adderley himself, the first Superior, slept on a plank bed – and was once prepared to give up even that to a poor sailor and himself to sleep under a rug on the floor.

Andrew's letters to his mother paint a vivid picture of the SDC in its pioneer days – and of the stark conditions with which its members had to contend. On one occasion, he tells her, he had to go and stop a man beating his wife and then to put him to bed. On another he found himself with a poor girl dying in his arms. Drunkards were a frequent problem. '"Mother says will you come and speak to father" is the regular message my children are always bringing me on Saturday night.' But Andrew remained cheerful amid the squalor and could reassure his mother: 'There is much to be thankful for, and I think a row with a drunkard does more for the cause of the Lord than a lot of preaching. The neighbours always take good care to let him know what language he used, and he is so ashamed of himself next morning'. Andrew compares the parish to a nursery of noisy children. 'The people come to you, two of them sometimes, a man and a wife, the one with a black eye and the other with a bite on the arm very likely, and they say, "Please, we've been fighting and want to be converted". Then you have to talk to them, and they shed tears copiously and kiss one another, and keep straight perhaps for a week, perhaps much longer.' There was soon a hard core of regular churchgoers – even on weekdays. 'Our dear people here are so good and the church is so loved. There are twenty or thirty people in church every morning at seven now, and one often sees some poor patient mother kneeling quietly and praying during the daytime. The work of dealing with souls gets more and more a passion to me, the thing to live for.'

The community was intended for laymen as well as for priests, and no distinctions were made in regard to dress, duties or privileges. Lay members of the SDC, after taking their vows, carried on with their original trades such as watchmaking or printing. Indeed it struck one observer as a 'curious and instructive experience' to find a monk in his habit working at an electric printing press. It was hoped that eventually the community would embrace men from every trade and profession, with the object of showing that 'such works as that of the bootmaker, the doctor, the artist and the mechanic are no less works of God than that of the priesthood'. The SDC had soon developed an outsize social conscience. As an article on its origins declared: 'Living as they do in a district where chronic starvation and want are the rule rather than the exception, the Community has entered into the troubles and wrongs of the masses; and the same democratic feeling that endeared the monks of old to the people marks its members'. The same article went on to observe: 'There is no doubt that those who live in daily contact with the morass of human misery on which the structure of our industrial system rests, and who look at these things from a spiritual point of view, have often a clearer insight into what is wrong and what is wanted than those who are content to study the problems in a scientific way from blue-books and reports'.

An endearing account of the community in its early days was penned by Sir Shane Leslie in his autobiographical *The Film of Memory* (1938). After leaving Cambridge he had lived for a while with the brethren at Plaistow ('the dearest of men'), so had observed them at close quarters. He recalls Fr Henry Chappel, 'the untidiest of the community, with cowl and bootlaces flying'; and Fr Andrew, 'a superb preacher who could really appeal to the men'. With the nostalgia of hindsight (and through his Roman spectacles) Leslie could look back on the pioneers of the SDC as 'real labourers in the vineyard bidding for the English working men, who now seem far from any church or Christian influence – beyond even the gentle counsels of Tolstoy or even the Divine Compassion'. He wonders 'whether the Church of England produces such types and characters now as then'.

Andrew's own religious stance in his early SDC days is defined in a letter which he wrote to his mother in October 1900 and in which he refers to the 'very illogical position' of holding extreme Catholic views about the sacraments and very broad Evangelical views about the love of God. Such a position, he tells her, is the only position in which he has ever found rest. 'Whenever I have tried for the love of you to be less "high" or for the love of others to be less "low", I have always lost the content of soul which is, I believe, a real symptom that one is abiding in Christ.' A month later he describes his present way of life as being not simply happy but positively rapturous. 'And yet it is the most quiet, tabby-cat sort of existence, in and out of the houses of the poor, quiet visits, quiet talks, a certain number of funerals. But the presence of God Who is so gracious makes life a perpetual holy day'. By this time the three founder-members of the SDC had been reduced to two with the departure of Adderley, who was succeeded as Superior in 1897 by Chappel – Fr Henry. The reasons for Adderley's quitting the SDC are complex. Kathleen Burne, in her biography of Andrew, refers simply (and diplomatically) to his 'withdrawal' from the community. T.P. Stevens, Adderley's biographer, defines him as a 'pilgrim always wayfaring in search of the light' (and adds cattily: 'His clothes suggested a pilgrim who had been on the road for many years'!). According to Peter Anson the view handed down in the community was that it was Adderley's vocation 'to be the founder but not to remain in holy religion'. Scott Holland once accused him of being a 'rolling stone' – in which connection Fr Reginald Wynter, who lived with the brothers in the early days, commented: 'He did not gather much moss. He seemed often inclined to diverge to new views and ideas foreign to his real convictions: he was not the kind of man to do a life's work anywhere . . . People often found his versatility bewildering and unsettling. But he lived the life and did the work he felt called to live and do'.* The fullest analysis of the reasons for Adderley's leaving the SDC is given by Barrie Williams in his *The Franciscan Revival in the Anglican Communion*. Williams suggests that Adderley differed fundamentally from his colleagues over the direction that the SDC should take, and that their conflict of views was not so much between social conscience and the religious life (as Anson had alleged) as between the religious life and the work of the parish. (A similar conflict was to develop a generation later

---

*On leaving Plaistow Adderley became Incumbent of the Berkeley Chapel in Mayfair. He subsequently held no fewer than six livings in London and Birmingham, never spending more than a few years in any one place – truly a 'rolling stone'.

between George Potter and his brethren of the Brotherhood of the Holy Cross.) During his rule as Superior Adderley had made three attempts to resettle the community elsewhere, but none of these had proved acceptable to his Chapter; so his withdrawal from the society he had helped to found could be seen as a gesture of protest at the recalcitrance of his colleagues.

Luckily for them, his departure in no way impaired the effectiveness of the community's ministry in Plaistow; and, under Chappel's leadership, it went from strength to strength. Its members won widespread tributes for their work during the smallpox epidemic of 1901–02, when they ministered to patients in the isolation hospital in Dagenham. They made an even more dramatic impact on the public in 1906, when one of the brethren joined the mammoth procession of the unemployed from the Embankment to Hyde Park. The monk concerned was Fr William Sirr, who had joined the society in 1902 and who was eventually to carve a lonely niche for himself as the solitary of Glasshampton. The march was featured in a big way by the *Daily Mirror*; and William, in black habit and cloak and surrounded by clergymen and unemployed dockers from West Ham, made a deep impression. According to Shane Leslie (looking back thirty years later), when the procession paused at Lambeth Palace, Archbishop Randall Davidson was too nervous to receive a delegation. 'At least he preferred to send a flunkey. We were not sure which alarmed him more: the Crucifix or the Red Flag in the streets.'*

William proved a great asset to the SDC during the fifteen years or so that he spent under its wing. He had gained practical experience of the life of the poor during his time as a curate in Vauxhall and found with the SDC the kind of community life for which he had been craving. One of his innovations was a series of Monday-night meetings dubbed 'Thoughts for Thinking Men'. Every conceivable subject that had any bearing on the

---

*Andrew's mother, when she heard about the march, wrote to her son in some alarm lest the SDC was being infected with revolutionary and socialistic ideas. Andrew wrote her a soothing reply and assured her that 'they all know very well what a Tory I am' and that SDC support for the march was a matter not of politics but of 'just simply desperately hungry men and women and children'.

realities of life, both material and spiritual, was discussed, though social issues predominated. The weekly gatherings proved an effective means of making contact with the men of the parish. William succeeded Henry Chappel as Superior in 1906, the latter continuing as priest-in-charge of St Philip's until his death in 1913. According to a memorial booklet published afterwards Chappel was a man of formidable, indeed awe-inspiring, virtue: 'He was a man of blameless and absolutely virgin life. His life had no dark chapter in it, one might say, no soiled pages. A teetotaller from boyhood, he had never known the taste of tobacco; he had never indulged the smallest bet; no profane or questionable word ever passed his lips. His interests were always wholesome, usually serious, latterly entirely religious; he had no hobbies, and despised holidays.' One may be forgiven for thinking such a paragon almost too good to be true!

*   *   *

Up till 1905 Andrew himself, while playing his full part in the life of the community, had, although a founder-member of the SDC, occupied a technically subordinate position during the superiorships first of Adderley and then of Chappel. But in 1905 he succeeded Fr William as Novice-Master and for the next two years enjoyed a semi-independent role. The society had purchased Potter's Farm at Stanford-le-Hope, Essex, to serve as a training-house for its novices; and it was here that Andrew took up residence. The house, while not too far from the headquarters at Plaistow, was then in the heart of unspoilt country. It lay in the midst of ten acres of land, from which barges could be glimpsed as they drifted down the lower reaches of the Thames on their way to the open sea. A dilapidated, thatch-roofed stable was converted into an oratory, while a poultry-run, orchard and vegetable garden provided for the needs of the refectory table. Besides serving as a training-house for novices, Potter's Farm also served as a retreat-house for missionaries on furlough and for the neighbouring clergy, and as a house of prayer for those who were too infirm for active work. As Peter Anson observed: 'In this little friary of Anglican Franciscans one discovered very much the spirit and manner of life of those solitudes in Italy to which St Francis himself loved to retire'. For Andrew it provided an oasis of peace after the rough-and-tumble of life in Plaistow. Although he missed Plaistow he appreciated the more relaxed atmosphere of the farm, with its greater opportunities for prayer and meditation. 'A sweet compelling sense of God's presence kept me in the chapel all the morning', he wrote on one occasion; and, on another, 'A day of prayer, still and peaceful'.

He was not allowed to savour the delights of Stanford for long, however. In the summer of 1907 the new Superior, Fr William, recalled him to Plaistow. The reason, he told his mother, was the number of outside calls for retreats and missions for which it was considered that he was better fitted than any other member of the SDC and which, because of his absence at Stanford, were having to be refused. 'If these are meant to be accepted, then someone else ought to do the work here, so our good Superior is going to change places with me.' But it was a wrench having to leave Stanford. 'The Superior thinks Plaistow is the place for me. *J'en doute*. God's presence is the place for me. Here I am at least learning something of my own emptiness and getting my pride mortified a little. Plaistow, I fear, means more of self and less of God, though that need not be and should not be if He sends me back there. As far as I can detect a preference in myself, the natural says Plaistow, the supernatural says Stanford.' He returned to the mother-house in mid-August 1907 and soon recovered his equilibrium. 'I am very happy here without the responsibility of the Novices', he wrote a few weeks later, 'and have been allowed to maintain the extra times of devotion which I got into the habit of at Stanford. I don't think my life can ever be quite the same again. Stanford was a new experience of what the life of prayer may be . . . I am infinitely contented'.*

The next major milestone for Andrew occurred in 1912, when he was elected Superior in succession to William. He was to hold the office for four years in the first instance, but assumed it a second time from 1924 to 1935. The procedure for electing a

---

*The friary at Stanford-le-Hope was acquired after World War Two by the Brotherhood of the Holy Cross and used for a short while as a hostel for homeless boys.

Superior had in fact been devised by Andrew himself in 1905. The electors were the professed members of the society, those overseas being allowed a postal vote. Superiors were normally re-elected for several years running to ensure a reasonable (though not permanent) tenure of office. But they had to go through the formality of standing for re-election each year at St Francistide (4 October).

By the time of Andrew's first election in 1912 the society was at the apogee of its influence. It was by now fully established as a religious community in the Franciscan mould. There was a steady stream of recruits arriving to test their vocation. Some left, but others stayed; and by 1914 there were as many as fourteen professed members, priests and laymen. According to a book on the society's origins, 'a great desire to share and sanctify the experience of the poor, to hallow commercial life, and to recognise the dignity of labour were the ruling impulses in the genesis of the Society, and it would wish that all its activities might always be biased in these directions'. The greater part of those activities, of course, were exercised through the society's ministry to the parishioners of St Philip's. The reputa- tion of the society was such, however, that its members were much in demand throughout the country as preachers, missioners and retreat-conductors. They had taken on the chaplaincy of the East London Cemetery as a 'corporal act of mercy'. They had acquired Potter's Farm as a centre for training novices. In 1914 they took on another responsibility: the care of leprosy patients at the Homes of St Giles at East Hanningfield, Essex – being assisted by the Sisterhood of St Giles, which eventually assumed entire charge of this work. But, in all their activities, they endeavoured to strike a balance between prayer and works. In this they sought to emulate the example of St Francis.

Two years after Andrew's election as Superior the First World War broke out, and the brothers soon found themselves in the firing-line. A number of bombs fell in the parish. The community house in Balaam Street received a direct hit, though fortunately no one was injured. When Andrew stepped down as Superior in October 1916 he was appointed Priest-in-charge of St Philip's, Plaistow. Apart from a year in Southern Rhodesia

(1932–33), he held the post till his death thirty years later. He acquired an encyclopedic knowledge of his parishioners, in some cases baptizing three generations of a family. He was available at any hour of the day or night to visit a sick parishioner or baptize a dying baby, and his influence and reputation became immense. A parishioner said of him once: 'He was like the ground under our feet and the sky over our heads. We never thought we could lose him'. And he was loved even by non-churchgoers, one of whom declared after his death: 'It wasn't only to the Church people he was a Father. He was a Father to all of us'.

But it was not only among his parishioners that Andrew established a formidable reputation. He was known far and wide as an immensely skilled confessor and retreat-conductor. One retreatant, comparing him with another conductor, remarked: 'Father X gives very good addresses and is a very good man, but when he leaves the chapel he is *gone*. But with Father Andrew you feel his peace and his holiness with you all the time, whether he is actually in the chapel or not'. He could easily have filled his time with outside work of this sort; but felt that it would be at the expense of the parish, so rationed his outside engagements.* He made time for a number of regular commitments, however, such as the annual retreat for priests of the diocese of Chelmsford which he conducted for many years at Pleshey and which was dubbed by the *Diocesan Chronicle* an 'annual benediction in the life of the diocese and beyond it'. But he spread his net as widely as possible, and was even prepared to address gatherings of public school boys. He made such an impression that one headmaster wrote to say that, on the Ash Wednesday following Andrew's visit, over two hundred boys had attended the voluntary service instead of the customary dozen or so.

And then there was the enormous number of letters he wrote, of which a selection is given by Kathleen Burne in the second

---

*In July 1944, at the height of the German flying-bomb campaign, he actually cancelled a priests' retreat at Pleshey. 'God knows how sorry I am to do that, and how very welcome a few quiet nights would be, but what my beloved people cannot have *I* must not have, I know.'

half of her biography. Some are addressed to friends, but the majority are to correspondents struggling with personal problems of one sort or another. In many of them Andrew reveals something of his own attitude to issues of faith and conduct. Thus, to a member of a Free Church thinking of joining the Anglican Communion, he writes: 'All Catholic Churches suggest God coming down to possess the souls of men: Protestant Churches suggest man striving to reach the throne of God. Of course, the two should be inclusive'. He rubs in the point when he writes to the same correspondent a week later: 'I was, you know, a Protestant once, and in those days my idea of religion was doing the best I could with the help of God. Now it is God doing the best He can with the help of me, possessing me and making the best of me'. On some basic issues of faith he is an unashamed hard-liner. To 'Mrs C.' he declares: 'People can be as original as they like in their ideas about the implications of dogma, but fundamental doctrine and dogma are like the letters of the alphabet, or the primary colours, or the scales of music: everything depends upon their static character. Other things can only be fluid with any safety and true liberty because they remain still and unchanged'. But he is no fundamentalist in what he considers inessentials. To the same correspondent he had earlier written ('my fifteenth letter this morning'): 'I have never wanted to think that the wet finger of a curate was necessary for a child's salvation. And it is that kind of attitude that repels me from Rome'.

Andrew remains always a good Church of England man. Thus, to a priest working abroad, he writes: 'If I became a Roman Catholic I should have to deny something I could never deny, my own sacramental experience; and I should have to affirm something I could never believe, the infallibility of the Pope'. But he accepted that the Church of England was far from perfect. To 'Mrs C.' again (with whom he kept up a correspondence for over twenty-five years) he reveals his special devotion to St John the Baptist. 'In my early days I think he kept me from going over to Rome, because the Church of England did seem such a wilderness. But it was to the wilderness John went.'

And he has plenty of good advice for those contemplating the monastic life, drawing on his own experience. To one testing his vocation he writes: 'Do try and give God a margin. Get up before you are called. Get to the chapel if you can before the bell rings. Never allow yourself excuses to stay away from chapel if you can help it'. Later in this letter Andrew tells the would-be postulant: 'Don't ever say to yourself, "Well, I am not a contemplative; that does not apply to me"'. I am quite sure that any true Religious can only draw water from the wells of contemplative experience. The real difference between the friar and the monk is that the friar takes the water from the well of Bethlehem out to the people: the monk pours it out before God'. To a novice Andrew can write encouragingly: 'I took my vows, and I hope if I had a hundred lives I should do the same thing again. My life has been on the whole a very happy life, though I never sought happiness'. Elsewhere he writes, somewhat tantalizingly, to a religious: 'My own experience of the Religious life has been that it began with ecstasy and went on to misery, and then it settled down to a tranquil peace and contentment which, thank God, I have enjoyed with very few ruffles for some considerable time now. I am quite sure that, if one perseveres simply, it is not only the most holy life but far the most happy one – only one must keep ever before one the beginning and end of it, which is personal devotion to our dearest Lord'. Finally, to members of a religious community, he gives some two-edged counsel: 'Always enjoy things. Then, if you have to give them up, there is the joy of real sacrifice'.

It must not be supposed, on the strength of these few brief extracts from his letters, that Andrew was dealing only with other-worldly matters. Some of his correspondents sought his advice on eminently practical issues. Thus he takes issue with a Free Church correspondent who had drawn up a rule of self-discipline which Andrew considers a little *too* severe: 'When you say you will omit marmalade, I take it that you do not mean to omit margarine too' [this was in the war]. 'I would not sanction that.' And he continues in very human vein: 'Personally, if there is one thing more than another I dislike, it is marmalade. I cannot imagine a bigger penance than to have to eat it, unless it was seed cake. Marmalade and caraway seeds are the two things

I have never been able to eat, try as I would!'. On another occasion he discusses with a correspondent (our old friend 'Mrs C.' again) whether she should give up smoking: 'You feel, on the one hand . . . disappointed that the desire to smoke seems to have got you into a bit of a bondage. On the other hand you feel that tobacco is a gift of God, and does you good on occasion, and that you ought to be free to use it'. After weighing the pros and cons for a page or so Andrew gives 'Mrs C.' grudging leave to indulge her passion: 'If you honestly feel that smoking helps your digestion, helps sociability, really tranquillizes you, helps concentration, use it, of course moderately. But, the minute it becomes an end to produce a sensation, then beware, and know that you are on the path that leads away from peace, because you are breaking the great Commandment, and using a creature without reference to and thanksgiving to the Creator, but apart from Him and His purpose in creating it'. Andrew cannot refrain from a plaintive postscript (and he was writing in 1936, forty years or so before the connection with lung cancer had been established and had begun to cause a sharp swing against smoking): 'I think you smoking people might just remember that there are people who loathe it. I hate the smell of it . . . I hate it anywhere and in any place and by any one. I think we who feel so *are* very considerate to smokers, and never object in words to what, as a matter of fact, we dislike intensely'.

*   *   *

Andrew's pen was not confined to letter-writing. He was a prolific author, publishing during his lifetime no fewer than eight books of poems and sixteen devotional works in prose. He soon established a formidable reputation in both fields – and even now, nearly fifty years after his death, is still filed under 'Popular Authors' in at least one second-hand church bookshop. His first book of verse, *Love's Argument*, however, was not published until 1922, when he was over fifty – though he explains in its foreword that 'writing in rhythm or rhyme has been a form of prayer with me ever since I can remember'. He sent one of these prayer-poems to a friend whose spiritual need he thought it fitted, and the friend had copies printed and passed on to others. 'That was the beginning of the discovery that my poor verses could be of help to other souls than my own. It is for that one reason they are published'. The successors to *Love's Argument* appeared at regular three- or four-yearly intervals, the final volume, *The Ways of God*, being published posthumously in 1946.

It is easy to see why Andrew's verses achieved such immense popularity. They have an unselfconscious charm which at once communicates itself to the reader, and an intensity of belief which can appeal even to those unable to share it. As a critic in the *Times Literary Supplement* put it, Andrew's humility and humanity 'transcend the limits of creed'. The poems were sparked by his devotion to the Divine love as revealed in the person of Christ and centred on three particular manifestations of that love: the Incarnation, the Passion and the Eucharist. They were full of pictorial images, the fruits of Andrew's early artistic training. Although almost all his ministry was spent in the drab environment of London's East End, the artist in him could see beauty in the meanest of streets and in the dreariest of surroundings. He had only to look at a child waiting by a bus-stop or a mother with her baby in a railway carriage to be able to transfigure the image by thoughts of the love of God. His feeling for his parish was revealed at its most profound in his only long poem, *The Tyranny*, published in 1940 at the height of the blitz and dubbed by Archbishop Lang 'your Hymn of Praise rising from our poor, battered East London'. Andrew himself described the poem as a 'sort of spiritual diary, a record of impressions and contacts as they came day by day'. Altogether, as a poet with a particular message for the English Church, he stands in the tradition of George Herbert and Christina Rossetti. That both his poems and his devotional works in prose met a real need is proved over and over again in the course of his correspondence. A priest in the outback of Australia, for instance, wrote to say that Andrew's books 'are a continual delight and a source of spiritual refreshment. I should like you to know what a great help they are to me, as they must also be to many other isolated priests all over the world'. And a priest in England wrote to thank him for his poems and to observe:

'When I feel "dry" in soul I sit down and read them; many of them I know by heart; often I quote lines from them in sermons . . . Your poems always bring one back to the heart of the Faith, the Incarnation, and that explains their beauty and power'.

Poetry was not the only form of art in which Andrew allowed himself to indulge. He never forgot his early training as a painter and made full use of his talents. He went around with a sketchbook and pencil in his case or pocket, and never hesitated to employ them whenever the opportunity arose. But even here his self-discipline was such that he would sometimes, as it were, combine business with pleasure by talking as he drew, thus making his pencil portraits an opportunity for spiritual contact with the subjects of his sketches. He shone as a water-colourist. During his holidays he would usually paint two or three water-colour sketches a day which he would sell in aid of one of his many charities. He was an amateur painter of real gifts whose work was admired by fellow-artists as well as by the general public. A rare tribute to his talent was paid by an East End factory-girl after visiting a room in which were hung twenty of his simple landscape pictures: 'It's like being in a church', she declared, though the subjects of the pictures were secular rather than sacred. At one time in his life he was misguided enough to give up painting for seven years, on the ground that it was inconsistent with the complete renunciation required by his religious vocation. Fortunately a fellow-monk persuaded him that this was one sacrifice too many, and Andrew returned with relief to his pencil and paintbrush.

He was equally hard on himself when, in the 1930s, he insisted on giving up theatregoing – another of his great loves. In a letter to Lilian Baylis, founder of the Old Vic and a personal friend, he confessed that there was hardly a bigger sacrifice that he could offer to God than 'the sacrifice of coming to the Vic as I used to. I believe there is no one who loves the theatre more than I do, or who is more completely happy in its atmosphere and in the appreciation of dramatic art; but that good thing God, I believe, asked me to offer up as a sacrifice and I have done it'. It was through his contacts with Lilian Baylis and other members of the theatrical profession that he was persuaded to try his hand at writing a Nativity play himself. The result, *The Hope of the World*, was hugely successful and attracted vast audiences. After two seasons at the Old Vic it was performed by his own parishioners at Plaistow – and was followed by a Passion play, *The Garden*, which was performed every Lent for seventeen years to overflowing audiences.

*　　*　　*

Meanwhile Andrew was continuing his highly effective but unobtrusive ministry as Priest-in-Charge of St Philip's. Conditions, however, had changed for the better since the SDC had first come to Plaistow. The lives of working folk might still be hard – but not quite so hard as before the passing of the National Health Insurance and Old Age Pensions Acts. No longer could the parish be written off socially as as slum. There was still poverty and disease to contend with, but no more mass-starvation; and epidemics were kept firmly under control. The easier conditions in the parish meant that Andrew could, with a good conscience, take a year's leave of absence to deal with a problem of a very different kind. This was a missionary venture of the SDC in what was then Southern Rhodesia (now Zimbabwe). Since 1926 the mission of All Saints, Wreningham, had been looked after by four members of the SDC, together with two women associates. The mission consisted of one white township and three native reserves. By 1932, however, the venture had run into difficulties, mainly due to a shortage of priests; and Andrew's object in visiting Wreningham was in effect to decide whether the work should continue or be wound up and put into the hands of the diocese of Southern Rhodesia. He made the most of his working holiday and came to regard the year he had spent in the mission-field as one of the happiest of his life. He wrote about his experiences in *My Year in Rhodesia*, published in 1933, of which the *Church Times* reviewer declared: 'He took to Africa the heart of a Catholic priest and the sensitive perceptions of an artist; it seems that he has left his heart behind him there, and his impressions have the vividness of a newcomer to a world of which every familiar aspect is a surprise and a delight'. Though by then well into his sixties, he had to learn both to speak the native language in order to make himself understood, and to drive a car to enable him to get around his huge new 'parish'. He surmounted both hurdles, though he found driving on African roads a nightmare and never derived any enjoyment from it.

A large part of his time in Rhodesia was spent in acting as chaplain to the lay SDC brothers and taking the sacraments to the Africans in their reserves. But he was able to acquire a thorough knowledge of the mission district and to determine that its care had best be entrusted to other hands, since the SDC could no longer staff it adequately. His year in Africa came to an unexpected climax. He had been billed to give a series of Holy Week sermons in the cathedral at Salisbury (now Harare), but was taken ill on his arrival there and was rushed to hospital for a major operation – which delayed his return home to England. During his year in Rhodesia he had made an immense impression on both Europeans and Africans. One of the latter wrote to him after his departure begging him to return – 'We chickens without mother'. He himself said afterwards that it had been the greatest temptation of his life to stay in Rhodesia and found a new community there. But of course duty to his colleagues at Plaistow was paramount, and Africa had perforce to take a back seat. At least he had some permanent memories of Rhodesia in the shape of the numerous paintings of people and landscapes which he brought home with him.

He arrived back in England in the late summer of 1933. His friends at once noticed a change in him. Lucy Menzies, the former warden of the retreat-house at Pleshey, was aware of a great withdrawal. 'He did not want to talk any more, and one always felt he longed to get away from all the multifarious calls and be alone with God. I expect the wide spaces of Africa wrought that.' Yet Andrew himself remained full of hope for the future. Only a month or two before his return he had written to his brethren: 'I count this year the richest year in my life, because it has been pre-eminently a year of prayer. I hope and trust that it means that I shall have a richer ministry to give to those to whom I am allowed to minister and a surer leadership to give to those whom I am allowed to guide'. In 1935 he resigned the superiorship to Fr Barnabas (Arthur Carus-Wilson) and was able to concentrate on his duties as parish priest. Four years later, however, the outbreak of the Second World War brought a host of new problems in its wake.

In the first place it raised the question of pacifism – to Andrew an agonizing dilemma. He was himself a pacifist by nature and conviction, but his fair-mindedness enabled him to sympathize with the non-pacifist point of view. 'I think England is true to England's conscience in going to war', he wrote to his regular correspondent, 'Mrs C.', on 4 November 1939, 'and I do not see what Chamberlain could have done other than he did'. Having declared his own personal position – 'To make a bullet, a bayonet, a bomb, is impossible for my hands that consecrate the Blessed Sacrament. I just cannot go from one to the other' – he came to the heart of the matter:

> But, having said this, I have not felt happy altogether in my association with the Anglican Pacifist Fellowship, nor have I felt I could join the Peace Pledge Union. I feel that many so-called pacifists are not really being true to their consciences, which are not so highly developed as to enable them to stand apart with Christ. If I detected them going into the wilderness for a time of prayer and fasting, and giving all their goods to the poor, and following in the footsteps of St Francis, I would believe in them; but I think they are not turning their own cheek to the smiter but the cheek of the soldier, who is a better man than they.

Later in the war (12 June 1944), in a letter to 'Miss P.', he wrote: 'Every Christian must be a pacifist, but I hold that every soldier is a pacifist whose whole intention is to wrest the bludgeon from the bully and to break it in pieces'.

Set as it was in the heart of London, the parish suffered heavily during the blitz – and its church was wrecked not once but twice. On the first occasion – 10 September 1940 – it was hit by the first bomb to fall in the parish during the Battle of Britain; the roof was split from end to end, leaving the walls standing up starkly and the windows gaping holes shorn of glass. The parish halls were destroyed in the same air-raid and left pitiful heaps of ruins. For the next six months the congregation worshipped in the nearby church of St Andrew. Although many of the locals had been evacuated, between six and ten people continued to turn up for the daily Mass and from thirty to fifty on Sundays. Andrew wrote regularly to many of the evacuee faithful. Meanwhile St Philip's church had been restored sufficiently for services to be resumed there at the beginning of March 1941. But its new lease of life lasted only a fortnight. On 19 March, during one of the worst raids on West Ham, it was wrecked by a landmine beyond all hope of repair. Not only was the church itself devastated, but the greater part of the parish was wiped out. Andrew told a correspondent in Rhodesia: 'Where there were crowded streets are now literally acres of moorland, with rough grass and undergrowth, wild flowers, and many goats tethered for grazing'. On this occasion hospitality was offered to the congregation by the matron of the Howards Road Maternity Hospital; and Andrew was able to carry on his ministry in the nurses' chapel there until his death five years later.

Throughout the war and the prolonged ordeal of the air-raids he himself remained a rock of serenity amid the encircling gloom. Indeed he welcomed the extra opportunities afforded him by the war. Thus, for instance, he sometimes found himself having to travel miles to a distant hospital in order to take the Blessed Sacrament to some evacuated member of his flock. 'I never wear a surplice', he told a correspondent, 'but carry the Most Holy under my habit. To me there is a very real ritual in this absence of ritual; and, as I sit in a bus or a train with my Lord resting on my heart, I secretly give benediction to the people I am travelling with and meditate on the words, "There standeth One among you Whom you know not"'. He rapidly acquired a reputation for complete fearlessness in the midst of danger as he comforted the sick and bereaved and led prayers in the shelters. One young mother, whose baby had been born during a particularly severe raid, sent a message to him as he lay dying in hospital: 'Give Father my love, and tell him I could never have got through that night if it hadn't been for him'. And an ambulance-driver paid tribute to Andrew's calming effect:

We knew that Father Andrew's serenity was the real, heaven-sent thing, and it comforted us more than any number of exhortations could have done. Nothing seemed to ruffle it. I remember one morning, at ten o'clock Mass, when the thunderous crash of a nearby rocket made us all leap in our seats till it seemed as if the very chapel had left the ground, chairs and all. But Father Andrew's quiet voice had not even faltered. He was so engrossed in the point he was trying to make clear to us in his brief sermon that it is possible he scarcely heard the noise!

Remarkably similar testimony was paid during the war (as will be seen) to the serenity under fire of both Brother Douglas and Fr George Potter. All three men struck observers as being totally fearless. But the war had taken its toll on Andrew; and in August 1945 (in the discreet words of his biographer) 'a surgical examination disclosed serious trouble'. He remained undaunted, assuring a correspondent a few weeks later: 'My body shows signals of rust and wear. However, I have had a marvellously healthy life as well as a happy one, and I am not going to let my mind dwell on anything but God's vocation for me, whatever it may be'. But there was a limit to how far even he could flog himself, and this was soon reached. In February 1946 he collapsed as he attempted to get out of bed. 'Apparently it was just temporary heart-tiredness which resented the extra effort of a perpendicular position', he told a correspondent. He refers in the same letter to 'the growth', thereby confirming that he was in fact dying of cancer. He spent ten days in St Thomas's Hospital, making the most of his time there by drawing the portraits of his fellow-patients and by conducting short services for them from a wheelchair. He left hospital for the home of a niece in Hertfordshire, but after only two days there had to be rushed to Bushey Heath District Hospital with ominous symptoms. Even here, however, with death only a week or two away, he could still write cheerfully to a friend: 'My vocation is in no way interrupted. I have contacts with men that I could not have in any other way. I was very touched because, when the Sister said that when the bed at the end of the ward was vacant she would move me there to give me more privacy, my young fellow-patient, who occupies the next bed and had opened his heart to me, cried out, "Oh Sister, don't take Father Andrew away from me!"'. But he realized his limitations and sent a droll SOS to the St Philip's parish magazine: 'It is really kindest not to write to me, and on the whole better not to visit me. Visits to hospital beds are very much like seeing people off at railway stations. The dear folk mean so well and are so kind, but after you have got into the carriage they stand about and feel they must say something and don't really quite know what to say, and so the conversation does not lead anywhere'. By an ironic paradox, by the time those words appeared in the April issue of the magazine, Andrew was dead.

On Saturday, 30 March, it had become evident that he had not long to live; and the last sacraments were administered to him. He died on the morning of the following day, Refreshment Sunday. His body was brought to the nurses' chapel in Howards Road on Wednesday; and, after Vespers of the Dead had been sung, the men of the parish observed a vigil throughout the night. After Mass at 6.45am the body was taken to St Andrew's church, where a solemn requiem was sung in the presence of the Bishop of Colchester, Charles Ridsdale, who paid tribute to Andrew in his address. A further tribute was paid at the funeral service in the afternoon by the Bishop of Chelmsford, Henry Wilson. The church was packed for both services. After the funeral, on a beautiful afternoon of early spring, the body was borne in procession through the streets of the parish to the East London Cemetery. There it was buried in a peaceful corner set aside for members of the society.

*   *   *

If this account of Fr Andrew has done nothing else, it has emphasized his formidable self-discipline and dedicated sense of duty. In an age when a person's rights seem always to take precedence over his responsibilities, the dedication of a man such as Andrew inspires awe as well as approbation. Indeed his 'goodness' is at times a trifle overpowering. To give up such harmless pursuits as painting and theatre-going for long periods of time simply because he considered that he was enjoying them too much: that would seem to carry the spirit of sacrifice to extreme, some would say absurd, lengths. Andrew did indeed represent the spirit of a sterner age than our own. Yet, that said, one cannot but admire such a wonderfully dedicated life which made so deep an impression on all those who came in contact with him. As one of his numerous 'spiritual children' remarked after his death: 'Every man, woman and child knew and loved Fr Andrew, and he was seldom to be seen in the street without a few children nestling under the capacious folds of his cloak'. Another observed: 'There can hardly be anyone living who will leave so great a gap or be so deeply missed. I think of him as the most purely loving person I ever met. There are other great intellects, other creative artists, other devoted workers, but only Father Andrew to whom anyone could always go and count on a response of sheer love'.

In effect the Society of the Divine Compassion died with Andrew. It lingered on nominally for six years after his death, but the heart had gone out of it. He had been its co-founder and remained its leading light for over fifty years. Its struggle to survive without him came as a forlorn postscript to the preceding half-century of endeavour. By now the society had lost much of its earlier impetus and power. It was without a novitiate, and its remaining members were a small group of aging men. By 1950 the numbers had been reduced to five and by 1952, when Fr Edward, the last Superior, died, to two.

It had been the genius of the SDC to hold in balance the twin ideals of the monk and the friar. Its members' life had its times of enclosure and retreat beyond what might have been expected of an active Franciscanism. Yet they wore the white rope of St Francis, manifested his spirit and sometimes his quaintness, and never failed in the showing of Franciscan compassion for the outcast. It was Fr Barnabas, the dominant figure with Fr Andrew in the second half of the society's life as Fr Henry and Fr William had been in the first half, who was sent to the then new Franciscan brotherhood in Dorset to take retreats and to advise them in the making of a new community rule. It was he who, in the declining years of his own SDC, favoured amalgamation with the Society of St Francis. So, when the crunch came in

1952 and the numbers of professed members had sunk to below the minimum required for a religious community, it was he who formally invited the SSF to send some friars to take over the work of the SDC. As a result of their efforts the foundation-stone of a new church of St Philip was laid in 1954 by Princess Margaret; the church was consecrated a year later. Brown-habited friars of the SSF now inhabit the house in Plaistow formerly manned by the black-habited members of the SDC. Andrew himself would almost certainly have approved. After all, not long before his death, he had commented to one of the friars: 'All that we had hoped for and proposed to do you seem to be doing'. So the spirit of St Francis lives on in Plaistow.

APOSTLE OF THE OUTCAST

Brother Douglas, SSF, in his old age

CHAPTER 2

APOSTLE OF THE OUTCAST

Brother Douglas and the Society of St Francis

A BRITISH SOLDIER serving in Hamburg shortly after the end of the Second World War was much struck by the sight of an Anglican priest in khaki uniform walking up and down the city's devastated streets giving cigarettes away to down-at-heel German civilians. The priest seemed bewildered when the grateful Hamburgers attempted to give him Zeiss binoculars or Leica cameras in exchange. 'I want nothing', Brother Douglas used to tell them; and, for the soldier-observer, this phrase summed up the saintly life of the co-founder of the Society of St Francis.

What was the driving force which impelled this gentle but inflexible man to throw in his lot with the flotsam and jetsam of society and to emerge as a champion of the underdog? In the words of his close friend, George Seaver, Douglas was a man of cultivated mind and cultured tastes whose company would have graced a senior common-room and one who appreciated to the full the civilized amenities of life. Yet he deliberately cut himself adrift from them. 'A lover of laughter and one who was quick to see the funny side of any situation, he identified himself with the world's tragedy as if it was simply a matter of course to do so. But in his compassion there was never a trace of sentimentality.' Seaver believed that it was, in the first place, temperamental and wholly natural, but that it was also informed with a simple sense of moral duty and kindled into a flame by a spark of the divine fire. 'He [Brother Douglas] was in truth a modern St

37

Francis by nature rather than by conscious imitation who lived from first to last "as poor, but making many rich; as having nothing, and yet possessing all things".'

*   *   *

The man who was to become Brother Douglas was born at Brighton, Sussex, on 8 April 1878 and baptized Robert Douglas on 6 May. Like Fr Andrew, he enjoyed a comparatively privileged upbringing. His father, Robert Percival Downes, was a Yorkshireman of humble origins who became a Wesleyan minister but, following a disagreement with the Methodist Council over eternal punishment, forsook the circuit system and began earning his living by his pen. He wrote a number of books, and was also the founder and editor of a religious weekly entitled *Great Thoughts*. Douglas's mother, the former Clare Elizabeth Trouncer, was an invalid – and, before his birth, heard the doctor tell her husband: 'Either the mother or the child will die'. It was suggested to Douglas that this prophecy, although mercifully unfulfilled, might have induced in him the tendency to depression which characterized his early years; and certainly, as the youngest child in the family, he was often spoiled and might well have been dubbed a 'mother's boy'. In a fragment of autobiography preserved in the Bodleian at Oxford he reveals that he sometimes told tales against his elder brother – 'and felt ashamed of my cowardice when I ran to him for protection against other boys at school'. Douglas's mother was an Anglican, and he sometimes accompanied her to worship at St John's, Upper Norwood, the district of Croydon in which the family had by then settled. The church was Anglo-Catholic, though in after years Douglas never fitted neatly into any ecclesiastical pigeon-hole.

His father's literary labours evidently made him enough money to enable him to educate his children privately. Douglas was sent first to Central Hall Preparatory School, where the headmaster used once or twice a week to give a talk to the whole school at morning prayers. 'I was inspired by what he told me about the adventures of missionaries – and believe I determined when aged eleven that I would be one some day.' At his public school,

Dulwich College, Douglas was placed in the form below 'a tall youth, Ernest Shackleton' – the future explorer. A great source of inspiration to him at this time was the life of St Francis of Assisi. 'It was my hope that some day in the Church of England ... I should be able to follow him and join a Franciscan community.'

He was confirmed at Dulwich by the Bishop of Rochester (and future Archbishop of Canterbury), Randall Davidson, on 12 June 1895, two months after his seventeenth birthday. But what he describes as his 'evangelical awakening' came a little while later: at a Sussex holiday camp for boys run by the Children's Special Service Mission. 'I wanted to accept Christ as Lord of Life, but I was naturally a bit sceptical even then. The matter was clinched by what appeared an astounding miracle, the discovery of a watch I had lost and about which I had been praying.' He had vowed that, if the watch were found, he would accept Christ as the rock of his life. On the last day of the camp he went to Bexhill; and, as he was walking back, he saw something glitter in a dry ditch beside the road. It was his watch. The incident set the seal on his conversion – and delighted his father, who wrote: 'Often I could weep for joy as I think of my dear lad walking with his face turned towards God'.

In 1896 Douglas went up as an undergraduate to Corpus Christi College, Oxford. After a weak start he improved academically, his third in Classical Mods being followed by a second in Modern History. It was during his time at university that he first came into contact with tramps – or 'wayfarers', as he always preferred to call them. He used to assist at services conducted by members of the Oxford Inter-Collegiate Christian Union in a common lodging-house in the parish of St Ebbe, and was able to talk afterwards with the inmates who came to the services. It was also while at Oxford that he responded to an appeal by the well-known American evangelist, John R. Mott, for young men to work overseas – which meant signing the pledge of the Students' Volunteer Missionary Union to go abroad for a few years. In Douglas's case his response came as the result of another 'miracle'.

He was keen on rowing, and had been given a place on the

bow side of his college's first four – but after a fortnight was displaced. There was a strict rule that, once a man had been removed from the boat, he should not be asked to row again. Nevertheless Douglas vowed that, if he *were* by some remote chance to be invited back into the boat, and if the boat then went to the head of the river in the bumping races, he would sign the SVMU pledge. He prayed for a week for the boat-club rule to be broken – and, a few days before the races, was asked by the captain of boats to take the place of a man on the bow side who had had suddenly to withdraw. The Corpus boat, by a series of lucky chances, then went to the head of the river. Douglas determined to sign the pledge. But first he had to read for ordination.

In the autumn of 1900 he began studying at Wycliffe Hall, the Evangelical theological college in Oxford, but after his first year there felt the need for more time in which to think out his position intellectually. In later life he was dubbed a 'liberal Catholic-Evangelical', with the accent strongly on 'liberal'. He could also be described as an old-fashioned Modernist, as he was always a keen student of the Higher Criticism of the Bible. He was in fact in the line of the mystics, a line transcending all the barriers of ecclesiastical partisanship. As a Franciscan he turned out to be neither traditionalist nor ritualist, but a combination of intellectual sceptic and practical mystic. He was a most devout sacramentalist. His loyalty to the Church and its prescribed ritual was undoubted, and yet his questing, speculative mind was never bound to formulas. But this is to anticipate. At Wycliffe Douglas had difficulty in resolving his honest doubts about certain aspects of the Christian faith and was unable to share the unquestioning attitude of his fellow-ordinands. Nevertheless, he was on the point of accepting a curacy at Hampstead when he was offered a job as tutor to the son of a wealthy American exporter of carpets residing at Smyrna in Turkey. In spite of a warning from his father that, 'if you do not enter the Church now, you will have to enter it some day or be a stranger to repose', he accepted the tutorship and set off for Smyrna. After some pleasantly relaxing months there (though he was once nearly kidnapped by brigands while out playing golf), he

returned home to take up another temporary job as master in a
preparatory school.

By now his remaining doubts about ordination had been
resolved. He was made deacon in 1903 by the Suffragan Bishop
of Barking to a title at St Mary's, Walthamstow, and priested by
the Bishop of St Albans the following year. His three years at
Walthamstow were uneventful. When he left in 1906 to take up
a second curacy at All Saints', Lambeth, his vicar wrote: 'The
relations between us have been most cordial, without a cloud of
any kind'.

The new parish provided far more of a challenge. It served a
poor working-class area, with six Sunday schools between them
catering for nearly three thousand children. The vicar, Canon
Allen Edwards, was a prominent Evangelical who treated his
four curates as his equals – which made for a happy atmosphere.
There was one point at issue, however, between him and Douglas: living conditions. Douglas felt the need to identify himself
more closely with the poorer parishioners, so asked for his
stipend of £140 a year to be halved. 'Don't be a chump!' the
vicar replied unhelpfully. Nor did he encourage his new curate's
wish to exchange his comfortable middle-class lodgings for
somewhere less salubrious. In the end Douglas found himself
two unfurnished rooms at the top of a working-class house and
moved into them without the vicar's knowledge. He furnished
them with packing-cases and orange-boxes. He was able to
entertain homeless men and lads here without having to feel
ashamed about his bourgeois surroundings. 'I found at once a
new joy in my work', he said later. 'It was as if a bright sun had
come out after a long day of gloom.'

The parish as a whole soon learned to love Douglas and the
children took him to their hearts, claiming him as one of
themselves – his guileless eyes always shone with the light of
childhood's candour. He usually travelled the streets at a rapid
pace, from time to time looking towards the horizon as though
he were following a star: some vision was urging him on, and he
was anxious not to miss the mark. As a preacher he proved
acceptable for his simple, heart-to-heart talks. But he had no
taste for preaching in those days, nor any faith in his ability as a

preacher – a feeling that was shared by his vicar. When pressed by George Seaver for reminiscences of his early life, all Douglas would reveal was that Canon Edwards, 'a man of experience and an unerring judge of men', had once said to him: 'Well, whatever else you'll be, you'll never be a preacher!'. He omitted to tell Seaver that, on a later occasion, Edwards had also prophesied: 'You, Douglas, will be the great apostle of the outcast'.

Before the apostolate began, however, three distinct episodes in Douglas's life were to intervene: work in a college in South India, work among the troops in Egypt during the First World War and work among undergraduates at Oxford.

*　　　*　　　*

The invitation to go out to India followed a chance meeting with a friend who, a few weeks later, was appointed principal of the SPG college at Trichinopoly. The friend asked Douglas to be his vice-principal, and Douglas gladly accepted. It was a golden opportunity to redeem his pledge to volunteer for missionary service overseas. He left Lambeth for India in 1908. His particular niche at the college was as a teacher of English and history: those who saw him in later years making jam or tending bees or striding the roads in the company of tramps would have been surprised to learn that he had once been acclaimed by a generation of Indian students as a professor. ('I always *was* fond of dates' was a favourite joke of his in the kitchen.) Once again, as in South London, he endeavoured to practise what he preached by living on the same level as his students, sharing their hostel with them instead of the comfortable living quarters in the college enjoyed by the rest of the staff. This impressed the students. The high-caste Brahmins among them, however, were less impressed when Douglas tried to enlist their aid in turning a piece of waste ground beside the hostel into a garden: to a Brahmin the idea of digging with a spade like a coolie was anathema, and it took a great deal of persuasion by the professor of history before at least some of them would consent to follow his example and engage in manual labour.

Douglas was responsible for the daily sessions of religious instruction at the college. He pressed the Christian cause with zeal, though he found it hard at times to distinguish between those students who were genuinely seeking after truth and those who merely wished to improve their English. He felt that Hinduism, after coming into contact with Christianity, was trying to purify itself and to read into itself Christian ideas which it had never before possessed. In a letter printed in the magazine of his old church at Lambeth he wrote: 'This process will, I believe, go on: and it is our part to hasten it until the breaking-point is reached and the old bottles of Hinduism can no longer hold the new wine poured into them'. In Douglas's philosophy there was no nonsense about one religion's being as good as another – he would have had little use for the present-day apostles of syncretism. In that same magazine article he had declared his belief that it was in Christ alone that India, split up by caste into a hundred thousand conflicting divisions, could regain that unity which was the first step towards anything like a revival of her past greatness. 'Politically I do not think she will ever be a great country; but spiritually, if she embraces Christ, she may once again be the leader and teacher of the world.'

During his six-year spell in India Douglas sometimes spent his holidays touring the villages round the college with a magic lantern and slides sent him by his old friends in Lambeth. As a means of home-spun evangelism his lantern lectures proved remarkably effective. But he also roamed further afield – and was tremendously impressed by his first sight of Mount Everest. He described this particular trip in an article he wrote for his father's paper, *Great Thoughts*. The glimpse of the world's highest mountain, he said, had been worth travelling 3000 miles to obtain – '3000 miles over the plains in a third-class carriage at the hottest season of the year'. Everest itself had a sublime effect on him. 'As we stood in the midst of nature's greatest temple, it seemed as though in the great white mountain we had seen a vision of God.' But not only nature seemed sublime. Douglas himself had made a deep impression on many of those with whom he had come into contact. Lord Lytton, a former Governor of Bengal, described him as 'the most beautiful and noblest character I ever met'.

*   *   *

Douglas's term of service in India came to an end in the summer
of 1914. At Suez, on the way home, a Muslim fortune-teller
assured him that he would be back in Egypt within a year; and,
almost as soon as he reached England, the First World War
broke out. Douglas at once volunteered for work as a Service
chaplain. But the Chaplain-General, Bishop Taylor-Smith, declined his offer and directed him to assist in his old parish of All
Saints, Lambeth, where he stayed a further year. Then fate
stepped in – in the person of an American friend who was
supervising the religious side of the YMCA's work among
Allied troops in Egypt. The friend invited Douglas to join him.
Douglas agreed, and was appointed chaplain of the convalescent
camp for British Servicemen at Boulac Dacrour, which lay on
the road to the Pyramids outside Cairo. He took up residence in
the summer-house of a garden attached to the palace of a
Turkish princess who had fled to Constantinople. During his
ministry from this unlikely base he prepared nearly a hundred
men for confirmation – out of a total of twenty thousand who
passed through the camp. Classes were held in the summer-
house, which was also the setting both for services of Holy
Communion and for rehearsals for the home-made sketches put
on in the evenings on a stage in the main camp. In the afternoons
Douglas often acted as a guide to parties of men wishing to
view the Pyramids and other local sights. Sometimes the sight-
seers would vanish to seek refreshment of a different sort in
one of the native liquor shops. 'How many sheep have you lost
today?', Douglas would be asked in the mess. One of his
favourite photographs was a shot of himself surrounded by
soldier friends at the foot of the Sphinx.

After a couple of years in Cairo he agreed to become chaplain
of a large camp near Heliopolis catering for men suffering from
venereal disease. He was standing in for an Australian padre
who had fallen sick, and the fifteen hundred men in the camp
would otherwise have been left without a chaplain. It was a
much less salubrious setting for his ministrations than the Princess's summer-house: the scent of roses and jasmine was replaced

by the pungent smell of iodoform. But Douglas found the basic needs of the men the same – and not least their spiritual needs. Once more he prepared men for confirmation as well as organizing impromptu concerts, and they for their part appreciated his faith, his courage and his friendship. One of his most spectacular successes was the conversion of a young soldier named Cooney who was locked up in a prison within the camp. He had no fewer than seventeen crimes on his charge-sheet, the most serious of which was killing, in a fit of drunken rage, a corporal who had been sent to arrest him; and he was described by a fellow-soldier as the worst man in the Australian army. Douglas had many long talks with the miscreant, discovered that behind the brutality and braggadocio lay much courage and unselfishness, and realized that here was a sinner ripe for repentance. In the end Cooney escaped being executed for murder by pleading (on Douglas's advice) mental deficiency in his defence. 'Mental deficiency wipes out all crimes', Douglas said later, 'and Cooney played his part in court and was sent to the hospital for the shell-shocked.' Douglas spent the last part of the war working for the YMCA on the Palestine front south of Gaza. On one occasion he was about to preach from a pulpit made up of ammunition boxes when an enemy plane appeared in the sky and a sergeant warned him: 'You'll go up like Elijah, sir, if that Johnny drops anything'. Douglas climbed down rapidly.

He really 'found himself' among the troops to whom he ministered. 'My best work was done in Egypt', was one of his familiar sayings. In the words of his biographer, 'it was there that he learnt what a persistent, prayerful love could do for the hardened sinner: a lesson that was to stand him in great stead in later years'.

*   *   *

It was while he was serving in Egypt that Douglas had first met Canon Edward Burroughs (later to be Bishop of Ripon), who had come out to conduct a mission in Cairo. He must obviously have made a deep impression on the missioner, who, at the end of the war in 1918, recommended him for a chaplaincy with the Oxford Pastorate. This involved him in evangelistic work among undergraduates; and he also acted as chaplain successively of University College (1919–20) and of Worcester College (1920–21). Recollections of his Oxford ministry have survived – and show the Franciscan Douglas in the making.

Charles Preston, who was later to join him at Hilfield and become a close personal friend, remembered him from his student days as a lanky, bespectacled man riding a shabby bicycle along the High and wearing a straw boater decorated with his college colours; a queer triangular bag of brown leather would hang between the bars. Charles soon got to know Douglas for his work on behalf of the homeless and unemployed. To Keith Davie, an undergraduate at University College and afterwards a member of the Community of the Resurrection, Douglas appeared at first sight to be a rather retiring and conventional Evangelical college chaplain. 'But we soon discovered three things: that our chaplain had a tremendous capacity for friendship, a grand sense of humour, and an amazing sympathy with the rather wild self-centredness of the young.' Douglas, in Davie's view, also possessed the gift of stirring others to share his own deep compassion for the underprivileged – 'and enlisting those who on the surface seemed the most unlikely people in the service of others rather than getting the most out of life for themselves, which was an only-too-easy philosophy in those post-war years at Oxford'.

Ronald Thompson, later to be Rector of Woolwich and a Franciscan tertiary, could also look back on his own undergraduate days at Oxford and recollect a 'very simple and unpretentious priest who seemed to find real enjoyment in being with us and who, even in those early days, showed an obvious delight in his fellow human beings and a deep devotion to our Lord'. To Thompson Douglas stood out from the general ruck of college chaplains as a man of 'many friendships and of much prayer'. But even then there was a considerable 'oral tradition' of appointments missed and other social derelictions committed because Douglas was so taken up with the person with whom at the moment he happened to be. There was one particular day, Thompson recalled, on which Douglas 'confessed to having had, for politeness' sake, to eat three lunches, having committed himself to lunch that day to three different people!'

In addition to his ministry among undergraduates Douglas devoted a considerable amount of his time to helping down-and-outs. In particular he assisted the Rector of St Ebbe's, Canon John Stansfeld, in building a shelter for wayfarers on waste land which Stansfeld had acquired on Shotover Hill, between Oxford and Wheatley, and also in constructing some little holiday bungalows for poor slum-dwellers in his parish. An account of the experiment recalls: 'The rector's "lung" at Shotover not only supplied breath to the people of the parish but inspiration to undergraduate volunteers'. Among the volunteers was Charles Preston, who remembered helping Douglas dig and level a road from the quarry at Headington and then to build the shelter for the wayfarers with gravestones from St Ebbe's churchyard. At the close of each day's labour the amateur builders would enjoy a bread-and-jam tea. Besides the shelter and the bungalows (in one of which Douglas kept three tramps for nine months out of his own earnings) the volunteers also built a chapel on the property which was used for services, retreats and private prayer. Douglas's involvement in the enterprise made a deep impression in the university. Ronald Thompson later recalled: 'It rather startled a generation of undergraduates, nourished on a rather sentimental *de haut en bas* concept of social service, to find that here was someone who actually, so far as he was able, *shared* the life of wayfarers. . . . I think that all of us who knew him then realized that here was a man alive with the love of Christ.'

Douglas's long hours of labour on Shotover Hill sowed the seed that was soon to bear fruit in Dorset. However (to switch metaphors), the spark that lit the flame came from an altogether different quarter – a chance meeting in the hop-fields of Kent between Douglas and a charismatic Irishman known as Brother Giles. Edward Kelly Evans, Giles's real name, had been born in King's County (now County Offaly) in 1879 and in 1911 had entered the novitiate of the Society of the Divine Compassion. But he soon became convinced that his real vocation was to tramp the roads as a friar and befriend vagrants and other outcasts. In 1913, as Brother Giles, he set out on his self-imposed mission, living in casual wards and doss-houses and sharing the life of the tramps. The hardships he underwent soon began to take their toll on his health; and from time to time the Cowley Fathers, under whose direction he had put himself, had to nurse him through bouts of physical collapse. The outbreak of war in 1914 soon led to a more prolonged interruption of his mission. In 1915 he enlisted in the Royal Army Medical Corps, serving as a stretcher-bearer in France. In 1917 he accepted a commission and served as a major in the King's East African Rifles. While out in Africa he contracted malaria. By Christmas 1919, however, he was sufficiently recovered to resume his ministry on the roads. By that time he had acquired his first disciple, J.R. Fox, who, after distinguished war service (he had survived the Battle of the Somme and been awarded the MC and Bar), was an undergraduate at New College, Oxford. Fox met him at the Cowley Fathers' church, and later remembered him as a slightly bald man under forty wearing a brown habit, a Franciscan cord and sandals. The two men got on well together; and Fox, later to be known as Brother Roger, joined Giles in the summer of 1919 on a mission to hop-pickers near Maidstone, Kent.

What manner of man was it who had so attracted the youthful Roger Fox? Writing with the benefit of hindsight over fifty years later in some 'notes' on the origins of the Brotherhood of St Francis of Assisi, Fox still insisted on Giles's basic charm while conceding the fatal flaw in his character. He recalled introducing Giles to his mother during a visit she was paying to Oxford and remarked that she was disappointed. 'Her common-sense revealed to her his lack of it. . . . Moreover, she felt too that he was Irish and in that case should be a Roman. His charm, in truth, did shrivel a little in her presence; I had to admit it. Yet I had fallen in love with my first impressions of the man and, still more, with the ideals which I had then heard expressed, so that it was to take a long time before the illusion was destroyed.' Fox thought that, as a solitary but saintly tramp, Giles might have risen to great heights but that, with the advent of a disciple, ambition may have entered his heart. 'It is one thing to protest against social injustice by suffering it yourself with self-sacrifice in charity; it is quite another to have the thrill of thinking you are going to found a new religious order. Giles of course did not see this.' But Fox was not the only one to be taken in by his surface charm. A.M. Lloyd, the practical ex-army officer who was to run the business side of the burgeoning community, was an unashamed admirer. Bernard Scott, a priest who spent six months with the community in 1922 after a nervous breakdown, recalled Lloyd's often remarking: 'Brother Giles is a saint. Just when things are getting desperate' (as they often did) 'he prays with such splendid faith that something turns up'.

But that was in the future. At this stage Giles was still feeling his way. His ambition to found a community of his own received a further fillip when Fox joined him, in spite of the efforts of Bishop Gore (prompted by Fox's father) to dissuade him. 'Brother Roger' was clothed as a Franciscan novice on 4 October (St Francis's Day) 1921. Among those present at the ceremony was Douglas Downes, who had already become acquainted with Giles during his visits to Oxford and who, at a fateful meeting in the Kentish hop-fields a month earlier, had persuaded Giles to accept an offer from the Earl of Sandwich of the lease of Flowers Farm, in Dorset, for an experiment in reclaiming wayfaring men from the life of the roads. Thus was born the Brotherhood of St Francis of Assisi – of which Douglas, by encouraging Giles to accept Lord Sandwich's offer, may rightly be called the co-founder. Flowers Farm lay between the villages of Batcombe and Hilfield, about four miles north-west of the much larger village of Cerne Abbas and in the midst of fertile farmland and the lush Dorset countryside. 'As I looked up at the coppice on the hillside', Fox later recalled, 'I felt I had entered into a novel by Thomas Hardy and hoped it would not end in tragedy!' There were certainly to be Hardyesque touches in the events that followed. For behind Lord Sandwich's offer lay an involved tale in which chance played no small part.

George Charles Montagu, 9th Earl of Sandwich, was the grandson of the 7th and the nephew of the 8th Earl. He had served as Conservative MP for South Huntingdonshire from 1900 to 1906, but by now had succeeded to the title. He was a practical philanthropist, two of his particular interests being the reform of the Poor Law and the treatment of young delinquents.

His family estates in Dorset included Flowers Farm; and it was there that, in 1912, he had launched an experiment in training delinquent boys and girls. The home was run as a self-governing and self-disciplining community by an American, Homer Lane, and was given the title of 'The Little Commonwealth'. Like so many idealistic ventures, however, it soon ran into difficulties and finally folded in 1916. Two years later Flowers Farm was taken over by Dorset County Council and run for a time as a centre for training demobilized soldiers in agriculture. In early 1921, however, the council had given notice to terminate its lease owing to the closure of its agricultural training schools, and Lord Sandwich was faced with the problem of what to do next about the farm. He toyed with the idea of offering it to some person or institution for activities similar in character to those of the ill-fated Little Commonwealth; but, in the absence of any such prospective tenant, he sent round a letter in March to various Church leaders offering the farm buildings and land to any religious community able to find a use for them. At first the letter fell on stony ground. The Roman Catholic Bishop of Plymouth, in whose diocese Flowers Farm lay and to whom a copy had been forwarded by Cardinal Bourne, wrote to Sandwich declining the offer on the ground that 'many of our congregations are closing down and leaving the country'. Another copy of the letter had gone to the Archbishop of York, Cosmo Gordon Lang, and he came up with the name of a possible tenant. He wrote to Sandwich: 'I wonder whether Brother Giles's ideas about a possible small community are bearing any fruit? I heard the other day that he was thinking of making a centre somewhere'. So Giles was by now known in the Church at large. Lang expressed doubts about his ability to undertake a 'somewhat large and responsible venture like this', but Sandwich was willing to clutch at any straw. He invited Giles to meet him at his home near Huntingdon and took to him at once. In September 1921 he wrote to him offering him the lease of Flowers Farm — for the first three years at a nominal rent. Officially the venture was to be a 'farm colony for such men as should be found suitable and likely to be benefited'. This was the letter that Giles showed to Douglas during their hopping

mission in Kent and to which Douglas advised Giles to reply
with an enthusiastic 'yes'. The die was now well and truly cast.
Writing to Lord Hugh Cecil about the venture in January 1922,
Sandwich described Giles as a 'very remarkable man who has
devoted his life to the study of the vagrancy question . . . It will
be an interesting experiment, and, although it is a far cry from
the Little Commonwealth, I feel it would be better to utilise the
place for it rather than just let it go'. The venture was to be
overseen by a small committee in Cambridge chaired by the
Master of Jesus College, Arthur Gray.

Meanwhile Giles had found two more colleagues. One of
these was Charles Boyd, an Australian who before the war had
tested his vocation with the Anglican Benedictines of Caldey
under Aelred Carlyle but had not joined the others when they
seceded to Rome in 1913; he had subsequently been a member
of the Anglican community at Pershore, but had not been happy
there and was therefore ripe for a move. The second new
adherent was Major A.M. Lloyd,, who, as we have seen, was
captivated by Giles's charisma. He had met Fox and Boyd by
chance at the Cowley Fathers' house in Westminster, where he
had been making a day retreat. They told him about Flowers
Farm, and he was at once swept off his feet. 'I have survived the
war with nothing worse than a limp', he exclaimed, 'and here is
your invitation for me to come and help you with this house for
tramps.' He and his wife took up residence with their two little
boys and a governess in the central farm building and provided
a welcome touch of what Mrs Lloyd called 'home comforts'
amid the Franciscan austerity.* Their Sunday afternoon tea-
parties were greatly enjoyed.

The first three members of the embryo community had moved
into the farm in mid-December 1921. They travelled by rail to

---

*The austerity was not all *that* severe – at least not under Brother Giles. According
to Bernard Scott the meals were 'simple and good'. Breakfast consisted of bully
beef, alternating with 'delicious cottage loaves' and margarine; lunch usually of
stew, with cold beef on Sundays; high tea of bread, margarine and home-made jam,
with large tin mugs of sweetened tea; supper of bread, blue vinney ('the Dorset
white cheese that is so like chalk') and fresh onions, with figs and dates for dessert
and more mugs of sweet tea or cocoa.

Evershot, the nearest station, and jogged over the remaining three miles of country road with the farm bailiff in a dog-cart. Word soon got around among wayfarers in the district that here was a likely refuge, and by Christmas the numbers at the farm had risen to sixteen. But it was too good to last. Giles was no organizer, nor was he able to make up his mind whether the place was to be a home for tramps or a Franciscan novitiate or both. By the summer of 1922 the atmosphere at the farm had become tense. Nothing that Fox or Boyd did could please Giles. Members of the Cambridge committee came down to try and sort things out – but, as Fox said subsequently, 'I was not of much help to them because of my loyalty to Brother Giles, or rather to the memory of him during those long walks and talks at Oxford'. Then came the moment of crisis. 'One day in September Brother Giles disappeared.'

The circumstances of his departure remain a mystery. Fox, writing fifty years afterwards, says simply: 'I did not know where he went, and I did not enquire. I think now that he went first to Glasshampton' (presumably to seek counsel from Fr William Sirr). According to Bernard Scott, who was there at the time of the disappearance, anxiety had brought on nervous depression. 'Brother Giles had to leave, and I think went back to Ireland.' Major (by now Colonel) Lloyd, in a letter to George Seaver (not precisely dated, but written after the end of the Second World War), is tantalizingly discreet. He tells Seaver that 'there is of course a considerable difficulty with regard to my stay at Batcombe [i.e., Flowers Farm], for it was there that poor Giles broke down under circumstances that should not be gone into'. Lloyd continues:

> The movement, which has been so wonderfully protected and nourished by God, was built on poor Giles's sweat and blood . . . Now no one knows where he is or whether he is still alive. I have written to the only relative I know, and she tells me that she has lost touch and has no means of finding out. As far as is known he had a job somewhere in S. Ireland in a golf club, but that was way back in 1924 or 5.

Giles's breakdown was probably due to a mixture of physical and mental causes. The intermittent bouts of malaria that he had suffered since the war may have contributed to his collapse, and the strain of directing the very mixed crew at Flowers Farm then proved too much for him. He would appear to have been more suited to sharing the life of the wayfarers on the road than to attempting to rehabilitate them in an alien setting. Nothing certain is known of his subsequent career.

His sudden departure threw the future of Flowers Farm into the melting-pot. His last word to his brethren came in the form of a letter bearing no address but dated 7 October 1922. In it he told them that, until matters had been settled, their obedience passed to the Warden (the Revd B.G. Popham, Rector of Tatsfield, Surrey). Major Lloyd would continue to direct secular matters. The letter continued:

> You will of course have the opportunity of telling the Warden, and whatever Priest-Religious is appointed to act with him, each one of you your views and wishes as regards your future. You will all of you make this a very special subject of prayer, otherwise God's will may be missed. I have no doubt as to the need of the life we have been aiming at, but experience has shown it must be conducted on different lines – it must be free from secularities and given to much more prayer. I see no reason why the work at Flowers Farm should cease.

The remaining brethren, Fox and Boyd, agonized over the future with Lloyd and even discussed it with their temporary guest, Bernard Scott, who recalled: 'Should we ask the Cowley Fathers to take it over, or should we try to find a new Head? We carried on after deciding on the latter course'. But who was to *be* the new Head? The Superior of the Cowley Fathers, H.P. Bull, thought Fox too immature and that an older and more experienced man was needed. According to Fox's own account he and Bull discussed possible candidates. 'We talked of the Reverend Douglas Downes, and he seemed glad that I knew him. He suggested that I should ask him [to take charge of Flowers Farm]. I went along early next morning and there came out Brother Douglas, his beautiful calm face expressing little surprise. He hesitated a short moment to reply to this request. He did so, and the Society of St Francis survives to this day*.' Douglas himself accepted the formal offer to succeed Giles with reluctance. 'I'm only taking this on till someone better steps in', he remarked with characteristic humility.

His inheritance was unenviable in material terms; and the Cambridge committee, considering that it was no longer financially viable, withdrew its support. Nothing daunted, Douglas carried on. As his biographer remarks, he was a genius at making something out of nothing. He not only found the annual rental for Lord Sandwich, but also repaid him the interest-free loan of £1,000 which had enabled the venture to be launched. But the farm was failing to pay its way and in 1926 was abandoned. The rest of the estate was given over to market gardening and various handicrafts such as weaving, basket-making and wood-carving. The later 'twenties were years of hard, unspectacular work while the new regime got under way. For the inmates it was a simple round of gardening, handicrafts, household chores and regular acts of worship. A daily routine was established, with parties of men working in the gardens, the saw-mills and the various workshops and breaking off several times a day for short, voluntary services in the chapel by the courtyard. Douglas himself would usually bring up the rear, hastening in at the last moment after a session with his beloved bees.

He normally worked in the fields or by the hives throughout the day. There were certain jobs, such as jam-making, which he reserved for himself. He acted as the community's laundryman, every Monday carrying out the weekly wash, and was also in charge of the cesspool. The care of the bees was his especial joy – he let them sting him mercilessly, as he said that it was good for his rheumatism. He became well known in the district as an

---

*Fox himself soon left Flowers Farm. He was ordained into the Church of England in 1925, but a year later became a Roman Catholic. He joined the Order of St Augustine, and in 1933 was ordained into the RC priesthood. He saw service as a naval chaplain in World War Two and spent the last half of his life at the Augustinian abbey at St Maurice, Switzerland. He died in 1987, aged 90. His autobiography, *Bridging the Gulf*, was published by the Amate Press, Oxford.

apiarist, and the locals would send for him to collect swarms of bees that had settled in their chimneys. In the early days the garden produce was taken by donkey-cart to Evershot station and thence by train into Dorchester for the Saturday market. Later the community acquired an old Ford car known as the Flying Bedstead which Douglas drove himself. His reputation as a Jehu was notorious. One wayfarer said that being driven by Douglas was like being driven through a cemetery – until you realised that it was milestones and not gravestones that were being passed so swiftly.

A vivid picture of the very early days at Hilfield* survives in a recently discovered letter to Charles Preston written on Christmas Day 1922. There is no signature on the letter, but the author was presumably an ordinand at Ripon Hall. Sitting in an armchair in the recreation hall in front of a 'roaring wood fire as large as any in an Oxford hall', he records 'funny old Downes' [i.e., Brother Douglas] as thumping out 'Mary of Argyll' on the piano. 'One of the brown brothers in his habit reclines opposite. The other is playing pontoon with three brother tramps. Both of the brown brothers [*who may have been Fox and Boyd*] are delightful fellows, and the brother tramps are just the sort of men I'd sell my soul for – outcast, homeless, lonely men and . . . almost all of them the "boys" that we kept the home fires burning for.' Some of them were disabled – which leads the writer to observe:

> Five years ago [i.e., during the war] they were the 'Mr Tommy Atkinses': now they are sturdy beggars and to most folk 'suspect'. However they are chummy fellows all and the friends of each other – there is never any squabbling, and I haven't yet heard a swear word! The spontaneity with which they call each other 'brother' would make the Ripon Christians blush. Really, Charlie, God lives here – you collide with Him round every corner.

---

*I use the term 'Hilfield' from now on to indicate the community's mother house, though in the early days it was sometimes referred to as 'Batcombe' after the other nearby village. After Douglas took over, Flowers Farm was rechristened the Home of St Francis.

This letter to Charles Preston was one of many which had been bundled into an old suitcase discovered in the attic of St Francis' House, Hilfield, during rebuilding operations in early 1993. Among the others were a number from Douglas himself to the future Brother Charles. They confirm that all was very far from being plain sailing during those early days at Hilfield.

Charles himself (1900–61) was a charismatic character. It was while serving in the trenches during the First World War that he first thought of entering the ministry, but the actual spur to do so came later. On demobilization in 1919 he entered his solicitor father's office as an articled clerk. According to his sister, Helen King-Magee, he was then sent to evict an old lady who was unable to pay the rent due on her cottage: not unnaturally 'this seemed to upset him very much'. He threw up the law and in 1921 entered the Knutsford Test School under F.R.Barry, going on to Christ Church, Oxford, and Lincoln Theological College. He was ordained in 1926. As both ordinand and young curate he paid several visits to the friary and took part in road missions, but for some years he was torn between the rival claims of a normal clerical ministry and life as a friar. Eventually, in 1930, he came to Hilfield as a postulant and the following year was clothed as a novice. He later became one of the best-known missioners in the Church of England.

An early letter to Charles is signed 'Bro.Wot-Not' and is dated 29 April 1924. In it Douglas reveals the tensions that were bound to arise in a community like Hilfield which had to balance the conflicting claims of 'faith' and 'works'. Some of the more traditionally-minded critics, he told Charles, 'tried to put us in our place. Told us we were no proper "Religious" because we sat loose to the vows of obedience, etc. and neglected the lengthy Offices of Holy Monks, etc., etc. We were even told that our methods were much rather those of the Jesuits than those of St Francis! I took it all lying down in a spirit of *meekness* which I hope was not tinged with *weakness*. I feel it very much to the good that those for whom Christianity *with frills* is vital have washed their hands of us completely'.

Six months later Douglas is reporting to Charles on a recent visit from the Bishop of Salisbury, St Clair Donaldson, in whose diocese Hilfield lay. 'From what the Bishop said afterwards I could see he (the Bishop) felt that the position of the Community was critical and its future dark unless we had the assurance of a fresh "move on" spiritually. This is only humanly possible (or even divinely possible for that) if we get some new blood.' Recruitment was indeed a problem. Douglas's most valuable reinforcement to date had been Arthur de Winton (Brother Arthur), a much older man of good family who had followed a career in banking with missionary service in Central Africa. The Bishop, Douglas told Charles, also felt that there ought to be more missions on the roads, – 'but how can two old crocks like de Winton and this child' [he himself was then forty-six] missionize effectively when the one day, Sunday, we are more than ever tied and bound? The work we do (in garden etc.) must be rather that of *supervision* than that of supplying extra 'hands'. We must think more of the untilled garden of God in men's hearts than of the weeds in the orchard!' In the end sufficient recruits (including Charles himself) materialized, so the community turned that particular corner.

A problem of a different sort occurred just before Christmas 1925, when some enthusiasts at the friary decided to go and cut down a Christmas tree for a children's party. Unfortunately they chose a tree on the estate of Lord Digby, a local landowner, and were caught red-handed. Douglas had to testify to the good character of the 'thieves' at Cerne Petty Sessions, but voiced his concern to Charles that the incident might be part of a campaign by local farmers to get the community cleared out of the neighbourhood. 'We feel we have been rather badly treated over the whole affair – which was exceptional and not an expression of the general spirit and tone of the men, which Lord Digby implied in his letter.' A bizarre twist to the affair was that Digby's aunt, Lady Lilian Digby, had been instrumental in securing for the community a promising new recruit, William Munns*, who, after being badly gassed during the war, had

---

*Another invaluable recruit who joined at the same time as Munns was Kenneth Hunt. He was professed in 1931 – and lived just long enough to take part in the diamond jubilee celebrations sixty years later.

been nursed in the field hospital she ran in France. Lady Lilian proved herself a staunch friend of the community – which was more than could be said for her nephew.

But even in the early days, when it was touch and go whether the community would survive, there were plenty of bonuses to make the venture seem thoroughly worthwhile. In May 1926, for instance, reporting on recent improvements at the friary, Douglas was able to tell Charles: 'We have so many pets – tame animals and birds – and their tameness seems to be catching. – I don't mean *tameness*, but their trustfulness and love. We have geese who can't bear to be without company and who walked upstairs to the landing to see where we were on Whit Monday when we were playing cricket in Frampton Park'.

In the midst of all his mundane work as gardener, beekeeper and laundryman Douglas retained a wider vision for his community. In a letter to William Lash (afterwards Bishop of Bombay) written in 1929 he envisaged a ministering order of friars – 'not folk living comfortably in well-equipped "homes" (we are to have electric light shortly!)'. Such an order, he told Lash, God would be able to use 'as a sword in His mighty hand for the overthrow of the kingdom of Satan – the curing of the indifference and unbelief, the sorrow and sin of the world'. Douglas enlarged on his idea in a further letter to Lash (9 March 1930). 'I can see an Order of Friars endowed by God with powers of the Spirit converting heathen England from the bottom upwards . . . I believe too that many a young man who wants to dedicate his life wholly to God will find such an Order just what his soul pines for. Not three priests but three hundred . . . is what I see!' Douglas defined the main job of his roving friars as being to conduct missions starting from the common lodging-houses frequented by wayfarers and spreading outwards to churches and chapels in the district. For, he told Lash, there was an ecumenical dimension to his vision:

> I see such a company of Friars doing for the Christians of
> England something of what the Christians of South India are
> hoping to accomplish – Union. The most marvellous thing I have
> seen, apart from the birth of hope in the eyes of the poor chaps

who come to us, is the way Christians of all denominations are
coming to regard and respect us. They come to our Chapel –
Baptists, Congrega'sts, Wesleyans – and say they love it, and they
invite us to go to their chapels. The walls that divide us are not
very thick . . . and the divided sheepfolds will become one flock
under one shepherd.

If this was Douglas's own vision for the future, how did
others view his existing activities? A revealing insight into the
community after its first seven years under Douglas's leadership
is contained in a letter (13 December 1929) to Charles Preston
from George Seaver, who was then in charge of one of the
hostels which had been set up to extend the work of the
community. Seaver was giving his impressions of the state of
the mother house at the time. On the spiritual side, he told
Charles, Brother Douglas and Brother Arthur 'are two of the
saints of God and they carry the atmosphere of heaven with
them. Consciously or unconsciously, the wayfarers are affected
by it as a consequence. No one who goes there who is at all
sensitive can fail to be impressed, and even astonished, by the
tone of the place – especially when he considers the contrast
from the life on the roads. It is like emerging from darkness into
light'.

Seaver was less happy about what he called the 'religious side'
of the work. He considered that the services in chapel imposed
somewhat of a burden on the staff [*Douglas, constantly interrupted
in his work among the bees, would have agreed!*]. He felt that for the
wayfarers what was required was a simple service of praise in
the morning before work, plus family prayers at night. 'Not that
I would imply deprivation of the Catholic Church offices from
any who really wish to attend them – obviously to Brother de
Winton and such as he they are the very staff of life. But we are
not all constituted in the same way.' On the 'moral' side of the
community's activities Seaver was cautiously critical. 'The brothers [*it is unclear whether he is referring to friars or wayfarers*] require
more supervision in their work and more individual attention.
Things go on behind the scenes which are wrong and could be
nipped in the bud with a little stricter attention to morality *per*

se. The pervading spirit of Heaven will not secure this in hearts that are not *prepared* on the moral side.' As for the material aspect of the work, this, said Seaver, was in a very bad state – but could be easily adjusted by employing a trustworthy manager of the whole 'interior economy' of the Home. 'I take no exception to the plainness of the fare, which is good and adequate – but the amount of waste is appalling, all for lack of a proper cook. Br Douglas sees this. Also it is no use making rules, or giving orders, unless it is seen that they are kept and obeyed.'

That was on the debit side. On the credit side was, first and foremost, Douglas himself. Among the archives at Hilfield are the unsigned and undated 'recollections of a man once young', which almost certainly refer to the early days of the community. The writer says that the impression Douglas made on a young man was of one entirely absorbed in what he was doing. 'To have any conversation with him in the day-time you simply had to do with him what *he* was doing in the garden or kitchen or wherever he might be.' The writer remembers that Douglas was full of ideas for the benefit of wayfarers as a group, as well as of the individuals immediately under his care. 'Yet he never seemed to impose his ideas upon you. If you entered into his ideas, he seemed to take it to be because they were also *your* ideas. It presented to me a new concept of leadership. He did not seem to have any idea of followers. If you went with him, it seemed simply to be because you happened to be going the same way. In his personal dealings this meant a tremendous integrity.' The 'man once young' recalls that Douglas would never expect you to do anything because he wanted it so, though he might help you to sort out what you really wanted.

> This made of the Home of St Francis a very real home, and everyone there on their metal to make the contribution of which each was capable. There seemed little distinction in practice between the 'brothers' and the wayfarers and 'guests' like myself. In the work about the place, in the visits to Batcombe or Hilfield on Sunday, in the going to market, the capabilities of everyone were called upon, and you could only sense the separate core of

'community' at the Offices in the tiny Chapel. . . . It was a rich experience for a young man.

In a letter to Charles Preston from which I quoted earlier Douglas spoke of the scorn with which certain traditionalists had viewed the unstructured religious atmosphere at Hilfield. These particular critics had pontificated from the touchline, but sometimes he had to face opposition nearer home. Fr Ernest Field, writing in 1956 about the early days at Hilfield, recalls a particularly tiresome thorn in Douglas's flesh. 'Amongst Brother Douglas's sins the greatest was that he used to be seen shaving within a few minutes of saying Mass in the morning; this was too much for the High Churchness of the other, who therefore abstained from attending Mass altogether.' But the critic was not content with mere abstinence. 'The men as they worked were fed with criticisms of Brother Douglas, and everything was made as difficult for him as possible. In face of this, together with the constant anxiety which such a queer, unreliable family . . . imposed, Brother Douglas kept his constant attitude of charity – "We must pray for him", "I am sure he is doing it because he thinks it right", "I must be very disappointing to him: I am so Low Church". To keep this charity constant under such terrific strain must have required supernatural grace of no ordinary endowment.'

Field also remembers the 'bemused kindliness with which he treated us youngsters, listening humbly to all our ready criticisms, urging us to join him working in the garden with the men, and saying nothing when we chose to do our reading and talking instead. It was his sheer goodness spread such an atmosphere that I cannot remember hearing even the mildest oath or hint of anything undesirable all the time I was there. The contrast between this and what we found in the casual wards was so glaring as to seem miraculous'. Field concludes his account with another impressive tribute to Douglas:

'Of course if you join us you may end in the Workhouse. But there is a lot of work to do for God there' was the oft-repeated warning. No one knew where jest ended and reality began, least of all himself – and that is perhaps the most vivid impression of him. He lived in the Divine Comedy – not God's Jester, perhaps, but God's Chuckler. He saw God's joke, that after all Love wins – and he proved it.

Douglas would then have been about fifty. A striking portrait of what he looked like at this time has been left by George Seaver in *Tales of Brother Douglas*. Seaver himself, after running one of the Franciscan hostels, went on to be Dean of Kilkenny and a distinguished author. He remembers Douglas as a 'tall, spare man in a capeless brown cassock, with benign blue eyes and scant fair hair, of open-aired demeanour and weathered countenance, the skin drawn tightly across a straight nose, wide cheek-bones and strong chin'. His brow was lined with horizontal furrows – 'sure mark of a sanguine temper, though in his case this might be also from a habit of raising his eyes skywards; or of listening courteously to a speaker; or simply because such is indeed the expression of the true field-worker'. Seaver goes on:

> His speech had an almost academic precision; his voice was cheerful, clear and gentle, but for all its gentleness it could be lifted in a high, authoritative tone. His wide, guileless eyes shone with the light of childhood's candour; and, when his ascetic features puckered all over with merriment, as they often did, it was with his eyes that he smiled. He had nothing of loud, robust, hail-fellow-well-met heartiness, but he radiated a spirit of geniality and infectious good fellowship. He seemed to be everyone's friend at sight, and yet there was about him a certain elusiveness and even a touch of inaccessibility, as of one of whom it could be said that 'all men count with you but none too much'. He seemed a mixture of enthusiasm and serenity, gaiety and personal diffidence; though vigilant and alert to all the multifarious activities of his Home, his manner was somewhat vague and preoccupied as he flitted from place to place.

Seaver enlarges on this vagueness when he goes on to consider the actual running of the Home. 'There was a total lack of organisation or of method . . . There was something haphazard and woefully disconnected about it all. For Brother Douglas,

intensely concerned with the culture of the inner life and himself
a model of self-discipline and unremitting toil, had about him a
strangely endearing vagueness as to outward things and a blissful
obliviousness to the flight of time; and this was often a source of
private exasperation to his colleagues! And yet things got done.'

Beneath it all Douglas was a man of culture and of cultivated
tastes. He was a lover of music and a capable pianist; and always
before evening prayers, which opened with a well-known hymn,
he would play for a little while from memory some passages
from one of the great composers. Chopin and Elgar were his
favourites, but by no means the only ones in his repertoire.

*　　　*　　　*

At regular intervals (about once a year), for days and sometimes
even weeks at a time, Douglas would absent himself from the
security and comparative comfort of Hilfield to sally forth for a
spell on the open road. His annual odysseys would take him to
casual wards and common lodging-houses in order to experience
for himself the actual life of his beloved wayfarers – the tramps.
By sharing their hardships he felt that he would be giving a
practical demonstration of the Church's care for the underdogs
of society.

Those were the years of the economic depression in Britain,
with over two million unemployed. On any day of the year there
might be as many as sixty thousand jobless men on the roads.
Under the terms of the Poor Law they were forbidden to beg.
When they arrived at a casual ward they would be given two
nights' lodging in exchange for a day's hard labour, such as
sawing wood or picking oakum. They slept squashed together
on rough straw mattresses on the concrete floor of rooms that
were little better than cells. The sanitary arrangements were
often indescribable. As George Seaver put it: 'Suffice it that they
consisted of a five-gallon petrol drum in the midst, and that it
did not suffice'.

Working conditions could also be horrific. In one letter to
Charles Preston Douglas gives a frighteningly vivid picture of
the casual ward at Church Stretton, Shropshire, in August 1925:
'The Master unlocked a "cupboard" (just like a dog-kennel I

had visited a day or two before), and there was a scarcely human animal breaking stones with scarcely room to swing his hammer. I shall not forget his face very soon, nor the faces of the other poor wretches who were breaking wood'. To the severity of hard labour would be added various personal indignities. On arrival at a casual ward a tramp would be made to strip and would be given a bath. His personal belongings would be removed and his clothes fumigated. He would then be sent immediately to his cell, where he would be locked up till the following morning. The food matched the living conditions: bread and margarine and unsweetened tea for breakfast; bread and cheese, or with luck 'skilly' (a kind of soup), for lunch; bread and cheese again, with tea or cocoa, for supper.

These were the conditions which Douglas insisted on sampling himself for days or weeks at a time. He would then have been in his late forties or early fifties. A tall, bare-headed figure in brown cassock ('my old dressing-gown') and clerical collar, he would stride along the lanes and highways in all weathers with head erect and eyes lifted to the horizon (as Seaver remembers), 'as though following a star'. When he arrived at a casual ward or lodging-house he would be an object of interested scrutiny: 'mingling with them, old and young, as one of themselves, sharing their miserable lot, dispensing apples and Woodbines (himself a non-smoker): this dreamy, picturesque and quixotic fellow, drifting in and out among them as if he came from another world, seeking the lost and lonely, warming them into life by his love, the infection of his good courage, the indefinable charm of his utter unselfconsciousness'. A fellow-friar, Brother Theodore, recalled in a BBC programme how Douglas used to look at people with those guileless blue eyes of his: 'They were a sort of childish eyes, more than anything, a child's sort of eyes. He used to look at one, and one felt that you daren't upset him because you'd make a child cry, as it were'.

But Douglas always managed to make the most of circumstances, however discouraging. In another letter to Preston, written in December 1926, he described a 'wonderful road mission tour' in South Wales in the company of an unemployed cobbler who had once been a champion boxer.

APOSTLE OF THE OUTCAST

I was a little afraid that he might let out with his fists if he had
to endure the 'contradiction of sinners'. But there was nothing of
the kind – it was amazing the welcome we received. As our fare
was very poor in some places, some of the down-and-outs wanted
to share theirs with us. In two Lodging Houses, with the permission of the Lodging-House keepers, I was able to address the
crowd – in one of them the keeper acted as a kind of Chairman!
The habit [*Douglas was wearing a grey cassock*] seemed to give men
the impression of one who had given up all for God, and it was
surprising how quickly they got down to the deepest things.

In a BBC interview recorded a few months before his death
Douglas referred to the 'absolutely shocking' conditions of the
casual wards in the 1930s. 'The smells, of course, were very
unpleasant', and among the worst pests in the wards were the
vermin – he caught seventeen lice on one occasion on one of the
night-shirts provided by the authorities. But even here the
charitable Douglas could discover a silver lining. On the morning after he had slept in a doss-house on Tyneside he was seen
thoughtfully scratching himself. 'Now', he exclaimed, 'count
your blessings, name them one by one.'

Douglas's work among tramps went far beyond sharing their
hardships on the roads and arranging for their rehabilitation at
the various Franciscan hostels he was instrumental in establishing
up and down the country. He set out to alert public opinion to
the appalling conditions with which unemployed men on the
roads had to contend, in the hope that the resultant outcry
would lead to a reform of the Poor Law. His practical experience
of the casual-ward system had given him an expertise on the
subject which no armchair theorist could hope to challenge.

In 1925, together with Major Lloyd and Mary Higgs, he
founded the Vagrancy Reform Society to forward his campaign.
Its aims were to press for the immediate reform of the casual-
ward system, to co-operate in redemptive measures, and to work
for their extension in the founding of homes for the training of
young casuals and in the provision of lodging facilities for
working men. Douglas advocated the adoption of the Danish
system of poor-relief. 'Just think of it', he told Charles Preston,

'when every tramp who sleeps in a Casual Ward costs the Rates more than a shilling a night. In Denmark all the first-grade Labour Colonies are *self-supporting*. That is a point that wants to be driven home. We are paying for the physical and spiritual degradation of men a shilling a day, and on the ground of "Economy" can't afford to save them and the cost of their maintenance too!'

Douglas's efforts through the Vagrancy Reform Society bore fruit. Under the Labour Government of 1929–31 a commission of enquiry was set up, and Douglas's evidence to the commission proved crucial. Many of its proposals were subsequently incorporated in a Vagrancy Reform Act which improved the system out of all recognition. But none of this would have been possible without the efforts of the Vagrancy Reform Society. As the 'man once young' I have already quoted put it in the course of his recollections: 'As far as I could see, the whole thing consisted of just three people – the Brother, Colonel Lloyd and Mrs Higgs; and those three, by gigantic bluff, changed the laws of England. I remember excitedly greeting Brother Douglas in Parliament Square after they had given evidence before a Select Committee of the House. Talk about David and Goliath!'

*   *   *

By the mid-nineteen-twenties the Brotherhood of St Francis of Assisi, the original name of Giles's foundation as inherited by Douglas, had acquired a written constitution. Its preamble recalled the objects behind the enterprise: 'to rescue the "down and out" men who tramp the roads (i) by providing a Christian Home for them where they can obtain work and recover hope; (ii) by sharing from time to time their life on the road; (iii) by training brothers for this work'. There was no endowment, but the work was maintained by the generosity of friends and the proceeds of the produce of the farm and market garden, which was carried on under the superintendence of a bailiff. The brothers lived under a 'simple rule of life'. * But, in its early days, the BSFA was an unstructured community – and the headquarters at Hilfield more a Home with some friars attached.

The welfare of the wayfarers came before everything else. When Brother Owen (Powell-Evans) was thinking of joining the community in the mid-nineteen-thirties Brother Charles (as Charles Preston had now become) told him: 'Don't come yet – chaos! We're only social workers in brown habits. Wait until Fr Algy comes'. 'Fr Algy' (Robertson) was Superior of the Brotherhood of the Love of Christ, a community run on Franciscan lines which had its headquarters at St Ives, Huntingdonshire. The process by which the two brotherhoods came together in 1937 to form the Society of St Francis was a lengthy one – and too complex to be described in a short biography. It has already been told in detail by Peter Anson in *The Call of the Cloister* and by Barrie Williams in *The Franciscan Revival in the Anglican Communion*. All that I need say here is that the merger came in the nick of time for the BSFA because, left to himself, Douglas would have neglected the interests of the community for those of his beloved wayfarers. In fact he was fully conscious of his own incapacity to assume the duties traditionally required of the head of a religious order. He was too unsystematic, too unconventional, and indeed very much too unorthodox. While capable enough when he gave his mind to it (as in his campaign to reform the vagrancy laws), he was no organizer. He was something much rarer: a visionary who could inspire others with his vision. He was also a genuinely humble man; and it was therefore with a feeling of profound relief that, when the two brotherhoods merged in 1937 to become the Society of St Francis, he could hand over its direction to one more suitably equipped than himself for such a task – Fr Algy.

When it came to running a community, Algy and Douglas were as unlike as chalk and cheese. Algy, like Douglas, was an attractive personality, with a fantastic memory for names, people, connections, etc. When he came to Hilfield he faced a very difficult task: to build a community out of a collection of

---

*The provisional rule of the Brotherhood was approved by Bishop Donaldson of Salisbury on 3 February 1927. Four years later, on 14 February 1931, he received the professions of Douglas himself (who took the title of Prior), Brother Arthur (de Winton) and Brother Kenneth (Hunt). At the same time Brother Charles (Preston) was clothed as a novice.

individuals many of whom had been accustomed under Douglas
to do their own thing. Algy needed to be a stern disciplinarian
and insist on order, otherwise the community would never have
survived. His teaching was solid, and his lectures and classes
helped to form and shape the new-style SSF. He welded its
members together to form an integrated group. Douglas, by
contrast, preferred to organize his own life. Under the new
dispensation he was Father-Minister and titular head of the
Society, while Algy was Father-Guardian, with responsibility for
running the friary. In practice Douglas left it to Algy to run
everything, even the regular chapters of the Society and the
Homes Committee, which co-ordinated the work of the hostels.
Douglas professed to be a figurehead and to leave it all to Algy,
whose method, efficiency and discipline at times frightened him.
He was a true friar, happiest when conducting missions or out
on the road. He was not much good on great ecclesiastical
'occasions' – which were meat and drink to Algy. In his later
years he came to Hilfield less and less often, because he felt he
might be in the way. He sometimes failed to see eye to eye with
Algy, though he trusted him and was content to leave the
community in his care. His general attitude can be summed up
in a remark he once made (no doubt half-jokingly) to Brother
David (who was to succeed him as Father-Minister): 'When I
was here we worked hard all day. You seem to do nothing but
ring bells and say offices – I can't think why!' It may be that the
enlarged community gained a great deal in the way of stability
only at the cost of something of that precious quality of simplicity which was Douglas's own special contribution. But that it
survived the death of its co-founder is in no small part due to
the stabilizing influence of Fr Algy. In truth the two men
proved a highly effective partnership in which their very diverse
talents complemented each other and were used to the full.

*   *   *

The Second World War, like the First, marked a high-spot in
Douglas's ministry. Once again it was the YMCA which secured
his services, this time for the chaplaincy of its hostel in the heart
of London. The hostel occupied the premises of the old Westmin-

ster Hospital (now demolished), which stood opposite Westminster Abbey; it catered for the needs of Canadian Service men and women and was tailor-made for Douglas's particular gifts. (It also took him away from Hilfield and possible tensions with the new-style regime there, but that is another story.) He always insisted on answering any call for pastoral help. One had only to give the password, 'Brother Douglas', to get past the Guardsmen outside the door of the hostel. He never enjoyed any real privacy. He slept on the floor in the chapel's vestry and took his meals in the men's dining-room. When he wanted to talk to anyone alone he had to do so either in the chapel or up on the roof, where he tended a kitchen garden and kept hens.* The soil for the garden came from St James's Park. Douglas charmed the head gardener into letting him help himself to as much as he wanted, and then organized a squad of assistants to take numerous sacks of earth back to the hostel and up the many flights of stairs to the roof.

He showed exemplary patience with the drunks and other importunates who tracked him down and kept him up into the small hours: sometimes he would let them sleep on spare mattresses in the vestry. He celebrated Holy Communion each day in the hostel chapel. He even asked the Abbey authorities for the loan of a chalice and paten and was horrified when they sent round two rare vessels encrusted in jewels. He took them back at once and exchanged them for a simple wooden plate and cup. He used to advise soldiers to go to the Abbey for the music and liturgy, and then to slip out to the Methodist Central Hall for a good sermon. But every night at 9.30 he would conduct Compline at the hostel or hold an informal service preceded by hymns – which he called his 'church bells', as they attracted people going past the chapel to the canteen. Those attending his evening services were given a cup of tea or coffee afterwards in his room; and the conversations that resulted would go on far

---

*One story that went the rounds was that Douglas had stayed up all night with a hen suffering from a throat infection – and that he had eventually cured it with M. and B. obtained by signing a certificate at the chemist's for his sick 'sister', Blondie Downes. But, according to Fr Francis's biography, Douglas had to come clean in the end to the chemist, who cured the patient with a drop of glycerine.

into the night. As Fr Stephen put it in an obituary tribute to Douglas in *The Franciscan*: 'Ordinary people of all sorts were attracted because of his gaiety, simplicity of approach, fearlessness, gentleness and humility. In him they seemed to find the real Christianity so often lacking in those who officially represent the Church'.

His fearlessness became apparent in the blitz of 1940–41, when he proved a tower of strength as a regular firewatcher both at the hostel and at St Margaret's Church opposite. On the night when the Abbey itself received a direct hit and the firemen's hoses failed to reach the fires in the roof he went up with some sailors and put them out himself at great personal risk. He knew the Abbey well and took parties round it almost every day, often working into his patter a short homily on some point of faith or morals. On one occasion a group of American soldiers, pleased with the quality of their guided tour, offered Douglas a tip. He politely declined the money, but accepted a new pair of shoes to replace the extremely antiquated pair he happened to be wearing. He didn't enjoy the benefit of the new shoes for long, however., as they were soon stolen by a thief who had wormed his way into the hostel. Douglas's reaction was typical. 'I am glad he took them; I was getting too fond of them anyway!' My authority for this sequel to the new-shoes story is Richard L. Brown, who saw much of Douglas during 1943 while serving in the RAMC at Millbank Barracks. Among other anecdotes he tells of one occasion when a man came to Douglas and announced his intention of getting drunk because of family trouble.

> Brother said, 'I wish you wouldn't because it will do you no good'. The man left, went into a pub, ordered a pint, put it to his lips – but did not drink it. Instead he put it down on the bar and went back to Brother, who had been praying for that man. When he came in Brother put him in his own bed while Brother slept on the chapel kneelers. Next morning he sent him on his way with a prayer.

Douglas's wartime ministry in London was interrupted in 1943 by an unexpected trip to Canada. It came through an invitation to visit the diocese of Victoria, British Columbia, with a view to setting up a branch of the SSF there. At that time it was difficult enough for a senior politician, let alone a humble friar, to cross the Atlantic, so how did Douglas manage it? Edwin Barker, who ran the Westminster YMCA hostel during the war (and was afterwards secretary of the Church of England's Board for Social Responsibility), asked him this question on his return to the UK in 1945 and received what Barker described as a 'historic' reply: 'I went down to the docks in Portsmouth and sat on a bollard by the water. As I sat there a young man wearing naval uniform and a lot of gold braid came up to me and asked: "Where do you want to go?" I said I wanted to go to Canada to visit some good friends there, so he said: "I'm going to Canada in my destroyer. Come with me". So I went'. Douglas was then sixty-five years old; so, whether or not he got to Canada in exactly the way he claimed, he was certainly embarking on an adventurous ordeal for a man of his age.

He landed in New York in October 1943 and travelled from there across Canada by rail. He was supposed to be merely 'prospecting' for a site for a possible Franciscan branch house, but before long was deeply involved in two vastly different spheres of work in British Columbia: as chaplain of the leading boys' private school in Vancouver and as an evangelist among the local lumber-folk. It had been suggested that the SSF might run a permanent mission to the loggers. Douglas had, however, been warned by his brethren at home not to commit the society too far at this stage of the war. This didn't prevent him from indulging in some evangelistic efforts of his own. He became firm friends with the loggers, though in the end (mainly because of a shortage of friars) nothing came of the Canadian venture. In the immediate future Douglas's services were required much nearer home.

In late 1944 Algy sent him a cable to say that he was needed in Northern Europe by the YMCA. He was considered an ideal man to minister to the spiritual needs of the Allied troops now pouring into Belgium, France and Germany in the wake of the D-Day invasion. It took some while for Douglas to wind up his Canadian activities, but he was able to sail for England in May

1945, only a day or two before Germany's unconditional surren-
der. In his final circular letter home from Canada he wrote: 'I
feel it right to obey the call, but I can't say how sorry I am to
leave British Columbia. My work among the loggers was still
only a day of small things, but the way has opened for future
developments'. In the event his mission had borne no immediate
fruit in the form of a Franciscan branch house; but his presence
for more than a year in Canada had made a remarkable impression. As one observer said of him: 'I have never seen in anyone
such clear and unmistakable goodness'. He was now about to
begin an even more memorable spell of duty.

It took him first to Belgium, where he served as chaplain to
the YMCA hostel in Brussels and then of a rest camp at
Blankenburg; but his most significant work was to be done in
Germany. By the spring of 1945 he had established himself in
Hamburg. The city was in a terrible state when he arrived there.
Three-quarters of it lay in ruins, and everywhere there were
hungry, homeless and crippled people, many of them refugees
and displaced persons from Eastern Europe. It was a golden
opportunity for Douglas – and he was not slow to grasp it.

At that time there was a strong wave of anti-militarism
sweeping through Germany: the ex-soldier, formerly so admired,
had become in defeat something of an outcast. The same society
which had fêted and honoured him in the hour of victory now
cold-shouldered him. Many of these ex-soldiers came from East
Germany and were unable to return to their homes. The disabled
among them had no one to care for them. For a long time
nothing was done even for the blind and the maimed. It was not
uncommon to see legless men propelling themselves up and
down the streets of Hamburg in crude little wooden carts –
boxes with wheels on them. In a single hutted camp at Harburg,
on the outskirts of Hamburg, a thousand men, all of them
lacking at least two limbs, eked out a miserable existence in the
nominal care of a single resident nurse. Conditions were appalling and the sanitation rudimentary. A doctor visited the camp
once a week.

It was in this hell on earth that, during the bitter winter of
1947, Douglas made his appearance. Leaving his comfortable

quarters in his centrally heated hotel – his warm bed, his regular meals – he took up residence among these outcasts of society in their makeshift quarters. He established himself at first in a wooden bath-house. He would get up at five in the morning to say his prayers. Then he would light his little stove and make enough porridge to last him the whole day – he could then let his fire go out and save fuel. To the inmates of the camp he must have appeared as a veritable angel of mercy. Dressed in a friar's garb, humbly performing menial tasks for them, sharing with them the major portion of his own scant rations, smiling, joking, always in seemingly irrepressible good humour, he completely won their hearts. The German warden described him as 'the most loved man in the whole hospital'.

Robert Birley, the future Headmaster of Eton and then an educational adviser to the Allied Control Commission, said that Douglas had, by his efforts, lifted an almost incalculable weight of misery from these men. 'This was the only one of those camps I ever went to of which I could only say that it was a cheerful place. He seemed to have discovered that this could be done practically without the use of language. I do not say that he knew no German at all. . . . But he could not converse. It did not appear to be necessary.' Birley added that living in Germany in the years after the war was for him, who had spent all his adult life in the sheltered world of the public schools, an extraordinary experience. 'Nothing was more startling for me than to find myself constantly faced with really appalling wickedness and really blazing goodness: wickedness of the kind one meets in Elizabethan plays, goodness of the kind one reads of in the lives of the saints. . . . Yet here I was . . . in the presence of a goodness which was simply destroying evil and despair.'

Professor Charles Raven, in the course of the panegyric he preached at the solemn requiem for Douglas in London, spoke of the way in which his ministry among the maimed and starving German soldiers had stirred the imagination and influenced the attitude of the victors and of the continental enemies of Germany. 'His work went far to challenge the widespread belief that there was no good German except a dead German, and to awaken the consciences of those who were living in

relative luxury among such terrible suffering. His example,
though he never realized it, went far to redeem the good name
of his Church and country.' By Christmas 1948 that particular
camp for the disabled outside Hamburg had been transformed
materially as well as spiritually: new buildings, reasonable rations, employment for eighty per cent of the men.

There were literally no limits to which Douglas would not go
in his efforts to help people. Once, when a legless man was
having difficulties in getting his pension, Douglas, who would
then have been almost seventy, carried him in his arms through
the streets of Hamburg and set him down on a table in the
pensions office, saying (in his very inadequate German) that he
would stay there with him until justice had been done. On
another occasion he took up residence in a civilian prison in
Hamburg. He had heard that the prisoners needed his help, so
he got into the prison and lived in a cell there, eating exactly the
same food as the prisoners: porridge, bread and margarine.
Edwin Barker, who had been sent to look for him, found him
sitting in his cell and feeding the birds with his meagre bread-
ration. These prisoners were, Barker said afterwards, the real
dregs of human society, most of them utterly conscienceless, but
Douglas was angry with the British authorities for their treatment of them. 'I have never forgotten his righteous anger. This,
he felt, was no way to build a peaceful world.' Douglas upbraided
Barker for refusing to make representations on behalf of the
prisoners to the Military Government. 'Knowing something of
Nazi Germany both before and at the end of the war, I tried to
reason with him – but his mind and heart were on the possibility
of a new Germany and on British attitudes necessary to this
redeeming work. I have never admired him more or agreed with
him less!'

*   *   *

Early in 1950 Douglas had a momentous decision to make.
Should he begin a new work of mercy among fugitives from the
Eastern Zone of Germany, or should he accept an assignment
much nearer home? The choice was not an easy one. He was by
now over seventy. Most men of his age would have been only

too pleased to sink into a well-earned retirement. For Douglas, on the other hand, it was simply a question of weighing one set of new demands against another.

By the end of 1948 his usefulness at the camp at Harburg had in effect come to an end with the vast improvement in its material conditions. Many of its inmates would have liked him to stay on and minister to their needs; but he felt that, if he was to remain in Germany, he ought to find some completely new task to tackle. After acting for a few months as chaplain at the British leave-camp on one of the Frisian Islands he felt increasingly drawn to service among the displaced persons from the East. But it was at this juncture that he received an unexpected invitation from a naval chaplain who had heard him preach to some sailors at Christmas 1949 and had been vastly impressed by his quality. The chaplain, John Armstrong, suggested that Douglas should come to Portsmouth as chaplain of the Services hostel there known as the Trafalgar Club. Whether or not to accept the invitation was the decision that faced him early in 1950. He passed it on to Algy, who discussed it with the brethren at Hilfield. Their reply was ambivalent.

They recognized that the Portsmouth job was in many ways cut out for Douglas and that, if he took it, it would be a joy to have him once again within easy reach of Dorset ('We all felt that we need a dose of your authentic Franciscan spirit'). At the same time they pointed out that Douglas had justly acquired a reputation as the 'Apostle of the Outcast' – and that the really outcast people were now the displaced persons. They agreed that Douglas would carry out the necessary work among young sailors at Portsmouth supremely well – 'but it was said by several members of the Chapter that sailors in Portsmouth could not be described as down-and-outs in the sense of those poor and needy people in Germany'. On the other hand, 'you may feel that in Portsmouth there is so much temptation and sin that these young men are in danger of becoming *morally* down-and-out'. The Chapter letter dismissed the argument of 'advancing years' as irrelevant. 'You seem as fit and vigorous as we have ever known you!' The letter ended by suggesting a typical Anglican compromise: 'would it be possible for you to set the wheels going in this new work for really needy Germans, and to come to England rather more frequently than heretofore?'

Douglas can hardly have found this letter much help in making up his mind for him. A clear directive one way or the other would have been so much easier. But the brethren at Hilfield understandably shied off from actually *ordering* their beloved Father-Minister either to stay in Germany or to return to England. They preferred to leave the decision to him. In the end Douglas took the common-sense view that he *was* too old (*pace* the Chapter's flattering words) to begin an immense new task in Germany. So he returned home to take up the reins at the Trafalgar Club.

The pattern of his life there – or the lack of it – was much the same as in all his previous assignments. There were no carefully laid plans, no effort at organization, no particular routine: merely an accessibility to all and sundry, a readiness to make friends. He slept in a tiny cubicle and took his meals with the men in their canteen. But old age was undoubtedly beginning to tell, and this penultimate chapter in his ministry was not an unqualified success – he was indeed wise not to have attempted a new and much more demanding assignment in Germany. To the majority of the sailors who came to the club he was little more than an object of mild interest and curiosity, and he was unsuccessful in persuading many of them to accompany him to the services in the Portsmouth churches at which he sometimes preached on Sundays: they complained that they were too dull. His own services in the club's little chapel were of a more informal character and attracted some of those with whom he had talked over meals. But he concentrated his efforts on deepening the spiritual life of the few. He conducted occasional weekend retreats and founded a communicants' guild with a simple rule of life.

Douglas's health really began to crack up in 1951. In the autumn of that year he underwent a major operation in Portsmouth General Hospital. This brought short-term relief – and encouraged him to take up yet another workload: at the Franciscan home at Goodworth Clatford, near Andover, Hampshire, which had been founded in 1934 as a hostel for tramps. He had been shocked to see how many of the sailors who came to the Trafalgar Club were suffering from mental illness of one sort or another, and he conceived the idea of making use of the Goodworth Clatford hostel as a convalescent home for such men. He moved there in mid-winter 1953, and for a time combined his work for the mentally sick with his Portsmouth chaplaincy.

The Goodworth Clatford experiment, like the Trafalgar Club, turned out not much of a success story: indeed, reading between the lines of Fr Francis's life of Douglas, one can see that it was a bit of a disaster. For once Douglas really had bitten off more than he could chew. He had blithely supposed that all kinds of expert help would be available. This was far from being the case. Indeed the Society of St Francis was so overstretched that it had no responsible person to send to assist him – and prayed hard that the venture would not end in total chaos. The fabric of the house was in a state of collapse. There was no staff and precious little money. Temporary helpers came and went. More seriously, the home in its new incarnation ran into local opposition. After a protest meeting had been held in the village Douglas had to promise not to take in patients direct from mental hospitals.

If the home was in a fair state of disarray when he was present, its state during his necessary absences beggared description. Fr Francis, who used to help there occasionally, has left a vivid account of one such occasion:

> Brother Douglas had left in charge a man who believed that all property and land should be free to all and sundry. Nothing therefore was ever locked up. Food and many other things, including even the lead off the roof, disappeared very rapidly. The cook was of French origin and had been a colonel in de Gaulle's army, but his cooking was far from French. A watery rice pudding was our usual sweet, coloured red when visitors arrived! There was a young man who would wander through the woods shooting witches with a bow and arrow; a man calling himself king of the tramps who visited many religious houses in Western Europe . . . paying his way by journalism and by playing a mouth-organ; and also an ex-friar minor of Maltese extraction

who was writing an abstruse philosophical treatise . . .

Such a sorry state of affairs could obviously not continue, and the experiment was soon abandoned. Goodworth Clatford ceased to cater for the needs of the mentally sick and reverted to an elaboration of its original role. In its new dispensation it provided shelter for three classes of inmate: the working man who found it hard to find accommodation in the town; the man who through some misfortune had drifted on to the roads; and the man who, through some temperamental difficulty, was unable to hold his own in the world. A warden was found who could turn his hand to almost anything, and the home soon took on a new lease of life. But the traumas of the last year or two had taken their toll of Douglas, whose health now began to go rapidly downhill. There are increasingly frequent references in his letters to 'Brother Ass' (as St Francis had nicknamed his physical health). Convalescing at Hindhead after a second operation, Douglas complained to a friend: 'Brother Ass was very troublesome at the end of last week – nausea and headaches – being in bed all the time makes him absurdly weak'. At one of the chapter meetings in 1955 he was in such obvious discomfort that Brother Charles was deputed to take him to see a specialist: the diagnosis was an inoperable cancer. He had a great dread of the disease, so was not told the news immediately, as it was hoped that special treatment could help alleviate the discomfort and prolong his life for several years.

In the event he was to live another two years; and, though increasingly confined to his bed, was still the inimitable Douglas of old, able to inspire and encourage all around him. Sometimes a discussion group would be held in the evening round his bed, when he would appear very much his old self* By Christmas

---

*Coleman Jennings, his old American friend, wrote from Washington in February 1957: 'It pleased me tremendously to hear that every night a number of people come for prayers in your room, and that on Wednesdays there is a religious discussion. I can close my eyes and see you in your bed, and hear your voice, and picture those sitting round you discussing things of the Spirit which you illumine with your little stories and your deep insights. It is something that these men will carry with them for the rest of their lives'.

1956 he knew that he was dying and wrote farewell notes on the back of his cards to his many friends. At the midnight Mass, clad in pyjamas and dressing-gown and propped up with air-cushions and bolsters, he presided at the chapel piano. He played and sang all the hymns and carols with his old verve, describing the service as 'the most glorious of all the services we've ever had here'.

His correspondence continued to be immense, and in his final months on earth his friends made no attempt to conceal their admiration of his achievements. The Bishop of Chichester, George Bell, wrote that 'many indeed there are who (for Christ's sake) will call you Blessed'. Norman Motley, the founder of the Othona Community, told Douglas that, together with William Temple and Albert Schweitzer, he had been one of the three inspirations of his life – 'and I thank my God upon every remembrance of you'. 'Tubby' Clayton, the founder of Toc H, told Coleman Jennings that Douglas was 'the outstanding Saint I know on earth'.

The end could not now be long delayed. By the summer of 1957 Douglas required more professional nursing than could be provided at Goodworth Clatford, and on 18 June was taken by ambulance to the Hostel of God, the home for the dying on Clapham Common. A fortnight earlier, ever mindful of others, he had written to a fellow-friar, Brother Patrick, 'I hope that after this last operation you may go on from strength to strength' – and had then quoted an African prayer: 'Lord, I'm a bicycle, but my tyres are flat. Blow me with the breath of the Spirit – and ride me!' In his own case the punctures had long ago been repaired – if they had ever existed. His room at the hostel was on the ground floor, opening on to the garden, and he settled down well under the care of the East Grinstead Sisters. One visitor remarked that the only place he could be happier in would be heaven.

In *Tales of Brother Douglas* George Seaver reports a conversation he had with him shortly before his death:

> 'How old now?', I asked him. 'Seventy-nine'. 'A good innings', I said. 'No, a long innings, not a good one. I have made many

mistakes – sent up many catches . . . The only thing I was really
any good at was in bringing the university students and the
tramps together . . . I have been such a muddled thinker. If I had
not spent so much of my time in practical work, I should have
been able to think more and get my thoughts straight.'

The chaplain at the Hostel of God, Maurice Bird, was able to
give Douglas Holy Communion every day, and also to read to
him and deal with his correspondence. 'It was this mail', said
Bird, 'which revealed something of the tremendous affection in
which this great priest was held by the widest variety of men
and women on whose lives he had made so deep an impact'.
One particular incident stood out in Bird's memory. 'Before
going away for a few days' holiday I asked Brother Douglas for
his blessing. In his humility he seemed quite astonished that
anyone should desire such a thing and, after giving me a most
beautiful blessing, insisted that I should then give him mine'.

Douglas had discussed with Bird all the arrangements for his
funeral and for the requiems. He was determined that they
should be marked by joy rather than gloom. The end came
'most peacefully' at about 9.45 on the morning of Saturday, 7
September, and Bird was able to offer a requiem for him almost
immediately. His body was cremated two days later in the
presence of only three people: Jennings, Bird and Fr Denis,
SSF. Douglas had wished to be identified in this way with the
many paupers he had known who had seldom had more than
one or two mourners to follow their bodies to the grave. On 3
October, the eve of the Feast of St Francis, a solemn requiem
was sung at St Matthew's, Westminster, in the presence of the
Bishop of Exeter, Dr Mortimer, Bishop-Protector of the SSF;
the panegyric was preached by an old friend of Douglas's,
Professor Charles Raven. Douglas's ashes were laid to rest
beside those of Fr Algy in the high altar of the chapel of St
Francis at Hilfield: thus, in death, the two co-founders of the
Society of St Francis were not divided. The interment took
place (after an all-night vigil) on the morning of 8 October in
the presence of nearly all the brethren of the Society. The final
instalment of the obsequies was a second solemn requiem sung

at the friary on 9 November in the presence of many of
Douglas's friends; the panegyric on this occasion was preached
by Dr John Moorman, the great Franciscan scholar who was
soon to become Bishop of Ripon. All that was earthly of
Douglas Downes had now been laid to rest. But his spirit lived
on.

*   *   *

'Already there is something almost legendary about him.' Those
words were spoken not recently but in a BBC programme less
than three years after Douglas's death. Indeed he had become
something of a legend in his own lifetime. I recall interviewing
him myself at Goodworth Clatford a year or two before his
death and being struck immediately by his transparent goodness
– not a wishy-washy piety, but an appealing mixture of courtesy
(towards one much younger than himself), serenity (in the face
of constant interruptions) and compassion for the underdogs of
society.

As Charles Raven put it in the panegyric he preached at the
first of the solemn requiems: 'The whole man gave an impression
of integrity and consistency: he seemed "all of a piece", possessed
not only of a single dominating loyalty but of a purpose so large
that all his several peculiarities of speech and action belonged
appropriately to its expression. In this regard he seemed to us to
be singularly Christlike'. Of course saints are sometimes difficult
people to live with, and Douglas must at times have exasperated
his colleagues by his blithe disregard of convention. For him
people always came first. But freedom to follow your fancy can
easily degenerate into the anarchic or the eccentric, and Douglas
had constantly to face the need to observe the discipline essential
to any community or co-operative effort. To his ability to do so
the successful emergence of the Society of St Francis out of its
two constituent and very diverse parts bears eloquent witness to
this day.

He had no gift whatever for administration, and his methods
could be exasperatingly haphazard. Yet, in the words of George
Seaver, 'he was an improviser with a genius for making something out of nothing and of converting the most unpromising

material, human and other, into the most serviceable use. Thus
he achieved more by the inspiration of personal example than
many who worked to the routine of a timetable could ever do'.
He was before all else a man of prayer. What might appear to
others as coincidence was to him providential. John Nicholson
(Principal of Hull University College from 1935 to 1954) once
remarked of Douglas: 'It is wonderful and unusual these days to
say quite simply, when a member of a cricket team is missing,
"Let us pray about it".'

Douglas's whole life, says Seaver, was an education and a
discipline in the practice of prayer. 'Life for him was an exciting
new spiritual adventure; every day held the promise of a new
discovery. His was the eager expectancy of a childlike heart.' In
an eloquent tribute to his departed friend Seaver goes on:

> To many people he seemed not only to exemplify the Franciscan
> spirit but to be himself a modern embodiment of the saint. Whilst
> it is true that he regarded St Francis as the highest ideal of
> Christian discipleship, he was entirely unconscious of any personal
> resemblance. . . . More apparent to others than to himself, how-
> ever, was his own strange resemblance to the Little Poor Man of
> Assisi: in his naturalness and simplicity, his humility and his
> passion for souls, his mirthfulness and prayerfulness; in his love
> of Christ and of men, of the outcasts and wayfarers and the lepers
> of society, of birds and trees and flowers and all the creatures of
> the wild.

To the closest friend of his later years, Coleman Jennings, one
secret of Douglas's charisma lay in the fact that 'he very simply,
effortlessly and positively liked his human kind; this gave him
the most inestimable gift which one person can confer upon
another – the gift of personhood, of respect for the dignity of
another, thus bestowing on that other a sense of worth and
importance'. The other secret of Douglas's life seemed, in Jennings's view, to lie in his understanding of joy – and in his
discovery of the particular mode of life which ultimately brought
him joy. 'To forgo the blessings of a family and home, to
renounce possessions, to spend much of the time in the companionship of people without culture or common intellectual inter-

ests, frequently to be the object of ingratitude from those he tried to help, oft-times to live in sordid surroundings with a diet of unsavoury food, in fact living his life under conditions that most people exercise the utmost effort to avoid – what a small price, he felt, to pay if this brought him the inestimable boon of living closer to his Lord.'

In the panegyric he preached at the solemn requiem at Hilfield in November 1957 John Moorman said that in Douglas could be seen the four marks of the true Franciscan way: humility, simplicity, poverty and prayer. First, he had had absolutely no desire for honour or recognition; all that he wanted was to be given work to do and in the hardest conditions. He attached no value or importance to his own life and, as a result, was indifferent to danger, sleeping quite happily under a glass roof in the YMCA hostel in Westminster during the worst air-raids of the war. Secondly, his childlike simplicity had given him complete unselfconsciousness, thereby unleashing powers that might otherwise never have found expression. 'It was not easy in the 1920s to present yourself for admission to a casual ward in a brown cassock; but it meant nothing to Brother Douglas because he knew that inside the ward were men to whom he had come to minister.' Thirdly, his greatest desire throughout his life had been to identify with the poorest members of society. It was this desire to be among the poor which had brought him to Flowers Farm, which had led him to tramp the roads and sleep in common lodging-houses, which had sent him to minister to disease-ridden soldiers in Egypt and battered and helpless ex-soldiers in Germany. Fourthly, said Moorman, the mainspring of Douglas's life had been his love of God and his neighbours expressed through prayer. 'To Brother Douglas prayer was such a natural and instinctive activity that he never minded praying for the most mundane things and always expected his prayers to be answered.'

But perhaps the last word may lie with Robert Crossett, who, in a broadcast in 1960, ended his tribute by declaring: 'I reject my superlatives one by one and can say only this: 'he was the most Christlike man I ever knew'.

Fr George Potter, BHC: a pencil portrait done by
an ex-prisoner

CHAPTER 3

POTTER OF PECKHAM

George Potter and the Brotherhood of the Holy Cross

Father Douglas was a man so good and kind
Someone to fill his place will be hard to find.
I hope your committee finds someone who's good and true;
I hope it's someone like Father George Potter, he's a good man
   too.

THESE ARTLESS LINES, written for the Society of St Francis by a man serving a prison sentence, are quoted by Fr Francis in his life of Brother Douglas. They could hardly have been taken seriously at the time by the friars assembling to elect a successor to Douglas. George Potter was then seventy years of age and a sick man – and, anyway, head of a 'rival' Franciscan society, the Brotherhood of the Holy Cross. But he and Douglas were very much birds of a feather in their concern for the outcasts of society, so it was hardly surprising if they should be closely linked in the eyes of those whom they had chosen to serve. And it was not only the two men who were linked. Their communities had for long been loosely associated in an informal way; and Fr Algy, for one, would have liked the relationship to have been made stronger. But in fact Potter was too independent-minded to be anything more than an uneasy bedfellow with the more structured friars of the SSF. He was basically a loner who preferred doing his own thing to doing it with others. The BHC centred on one man, Fr George, and that was its basic weakness. It did splendid work in a poverty-stricken parish in South London, but the traditional trappings of the religious life took second place to the needs of the parish. This was fine while George Potter was alive; but, once his charismatic presence had been removed by death, there was no one really capable of taking his place and the community soon collapsed. Nevertheless, for nearly forty years he performed heroic labours in his chosen patch; and the memory of 'Father Potter of Peckham' lives on to this day in South London. His story deserves to be retold to a wider audience as an example of what one man can achieve if his faith is strong enough to surmount the obstacles in his path.

*   *   *

George Potter came from a humbler background than either Fr Andrew or Brother Douglas. Not for him the comfort and security of a professional man's home and an education centred on public school and Oxford. George's father, also George, was a railway clerk by profession and so would have been categorized as lower-middle-class. He died in 1889, leaving his widow, the former Eliza Jeannette Favey, to bring up a family of five children on her own. George junior was the youngest child. He was born on 13 April 1887 at 6 Park Terrace, Balham, on the boundary with Clapham. Park Terrace was a group of houses in Cavendish Road; and it was there that George spent his childhood. At the end of the Potter garden was a much larger garden attached to a house owned by the famous comic actor, Dan Leno. On one occasion, George recalls in his autobiography, he narrowly avoided hitting the actor with a pellet from his airgun; but the encounter led to an introduction to the Leno family and to 'many happy hours' spent with Dan and his sons. The friendship led to George's subsequent keen interest in the stage.

Life was far from easy in Cavendish Road. Mrs Potter had to go out to work as a 'daily' to support her family, and two years after her husband's death three of the five children were already earning their living: the two daughters, 17-year-old Georgina and 15-year-old Eliza, as apprentice dressmakers and 14-year-old Daniel as a post-office errand-boy. The two youngest in the family, George and his brother Frederick, five years his senior, were looked after during the daytime (when not at school) by their grandmother, Elizabeth Favey. But George admits that his father's early death meant that he had more freedom than was usual for a boy of his age – but that, likewise, bereavement 'did much to develop in us a love for one another that drew the family closer together'. This close sense of family never deserted him. In later years he provided a home for his mother; and his sisters became two of his most devoted helpers after his appointment to St Chrysostom's, Peckham.

George was educated locally. He recalls an untactful remark made to him on his first day at St Mary's Infants' School, Balham, by the assistant priest attached to the church: 'George! You've got your breeches on the wrong way round!' But he speaks highly of his headmaster, Albert Sargeant, 'a man with a real vocation'. It may well have been Sargeant who helped foster George's own vocation to the ministry, which he says in his book first came to him at the age of nine. But at that stage it seemed to him no more than a pipe-dream – 'a widowed mother, no money, and what was then known as a Higher Grade School education (we dabbled with French and algebra)'. The need to help augment the family income led to his leaving school at thirteen and going out to work. He began in a private detective agency in Queen Victoria Street at six shillings a week, but after a few months progressed to a sugar-broker's office in Mincing Lane and thence to a stockbroker's office as a junior clerk. He toiled away at the stockbroker's for five years, by when his wages had risen to a pound a week. But all this time he was nurturing his vocation; and by the time he was eighteen his vicar at St Mary's, Thomas Bates, took it sufficiently seriously to send him to the Chapter-House in St Thomas's Street, Southwark, 'where two good young priests gave up three evenings a week to help youngsters like me to master the rudiments of Latin, Greek, the Bible and Church history'. Later he attended evening classes at King's College in the Strand, going there straight from work after a hurried meal of sandwiches eaten in the Royal Exchange. But even that was not the end of his day. 'Then I had to sit up until the early hours of the morning, trying to digest Greek paradigms and Latin declensions.'

This early version of the Southwark Ordination Course meant gruellingly hard work on top of George's full-time job at the stockbroker's, but at last it began to pay off. By now Canon Bates had been made rural dean; and he encouraged George to forsake the stockbroker and assist him in his secretarial work. The idea was to give George more time to study, but the time was never forthcoming. 'As secretary, parish clerk, verger, parish visitor, club leader, lay reader and whatnot', says George, 'my day began at 6.30am and finished after 10pm.'

George's dilemma was resolved when he happened to pick up a copy of Fr Herbert Kelly's *An Idea in the Working*. The book told the story of the Society of the Sacred Mission, a religious order founded by Kelly in 1894, and of its decision to train for ordination men who lacked the means to obtain a university education. The college at Kelham in Nottinghamshire seemed tailor-made for a youth in George's position; and, with Bates's good-will, he applied for admission in 1909 and was accepted. In after-years he looked back with gratitude to his time at Kelham. Life was tough,* but the material hardships were compensated for by the sense of fellowship and vocation and by the devotion of the priests and tutors. George was strongly influenced both by Kelly himself and by his successor as Superior, David Jenks. In *More Father Potter* he recounts a string of anecdotes about Kelly – as when in nervousness he dropped the pages of an essay he was about to hand in and the Superior observed: 'Oh, my son, don't trouble to put the pages in order. I expect it is full of tripe and heresy!'. George had his revenge afterwards when, as student in charge of the Gym Squad, he induced Kelly to climb along a horizontal ladder upside down. 'For days after he would hold his ribs and grunt whenever he passed me.' Later, when Jenks replaced Kelly, George was much moved to see the former Superior kneeling to pledge his loyalty and obedience to his successor.

Sadly, George was unable to complete the full course at

---

*The students had to take a primitive form of cold bath every day. Each student had to sit in a tub placed on the concrete floor by his bed while a fellow-student poured cold, often icy, water from a large jug all over him.

Kelham. He developed severe gastric trouble (no doubt brought on by the Spartan meals at the college) and had to leave after eighteen months. Gastritis was to plague him for the next thirty years and force him at times to go on a special diet. But he never allowed it to restrict his activities more than he could help. Meanwhile he had to complete his training for ordination; and here the ever-helpful Bates once again came to the rescue. He approached the trustees of the South London Church Fund; and they were able to find three anonymous donors who, between them, supplied the fees needed to see George through a two-year day course at King's College, London. He lived at home, earning sufficient money in the evenings to provide his share of the family budget. It was a hard slog, but in 1912 he qualified to become an Associate of King's College – his necessary passport to the ministry.

He was ordained deacon in Southwark Cathedral in 1912 by Bishop Burge to a title at All Saints', South Wimbledon, and was priested two years later. The parish was exceptionally poor in material terms. According to George it contained only three bathrooms – and the clergy had two of these. He was certainly thrown in at the deep end of parochial ministry. On one occasion he recalls hearing unearthly shrieks coming from a caravan berthed on waste ground. 'I pushed my way in and found a man holding on to a woman's hair as he slashed her with his belt. I went up and pushed him away. I turned to the woman to inquire whether she was hurt, when she pushed *me* away, saying: "You git out of it; he's my man! Let him do as he likes!"'

On another occasion only presence of mind saved George from what might well have developed into a nasty situation. He had been summoned by a small boy to call on his mother, who was alleged to be very ill. On being admitted to the house he was pushed into a darkened and apparently empty room and heard the key turned in the lock. He shouted, 'Is anybody here?', and eventually a light went on and a woman in 'scanty deshabille' came out and glared at him. The sequel must be told in George's own words:

I asked what she wanted. She put her arms round me and said, 'I
want you!', and started to slobber over me. Remember, I'd only
been priested a few months, but I was evidently worldly-wise
enough to know what might have happened. I even imagined
myself in a police-court, faced with all kinds of evil accusations. I
gave her a hefty punch, and she curled up under the piano.

The door was still locked, but George managed to escape
through a window. 'I realize now that, if I had stayed longer, a
"shocked" husband would have unlocked the door and wanted
to know what was going on.'

Even 'normal' sick visiting had its unusual moments. Once,
when George went to call on an invalid, he found the house in
darkness and the patient dead and, on going out to summon
assistance, tripped over another corpse in the passage. 'Later I
learnt that the second body was that of a relative who had
visited the sick man and who, like me, had been surprised, to
say the least of it. His heart was evidently weaker than mine.'

Half-way through George's time at Wimbledon the First
World War broke out, and in due course he enlisted as an army
chaplain. We know little of how he spent his year in uniform,
except that it was divided between France and Egypt. But his
experiences on the Western Front taught him to appreciate the
simple things connected with worship:

> There was something rather thrilling in sheltering under a tree in
> France with an altar made of a couple of boxes of bombs. On one
> occasion I remember having to use a tin mug and plate at the
> Mass, as my groom had lost his way ... There was no time or
> opportunity for much elaborate ceremonial. I learnt many things
> worth knowing – among them I learnt to be careful in genuflecting
> if one was wearing spurs.

It was while he was in Egypt that George first met Brother
Douglas, who was then ministering to British Servicemen at the
convalescent camp outside Cairo. But his stay in Egypt was
brief. In 1917 recurring attacks of gastritis led to his returning
home to take up a curacy at St Bartholomew's, Bermondsey,
under Canon George Branson. The parish was similar in type to

All Saints', South Wimbledon, and George found himself in similarly tough situations. On one occasion he appeared in the pulpit with a black eye and one arm in a sling. 'I had had a few words and an exchange of punches with a hefty Billingsgate porter, and he had fists like slabs of concrete.' On another occasion he found a drunken woman lying in the gutter, dragged her to her feet and poured a jug of cold water over her. Her husband had been shouting abuse at her, but George threatened him with similar treatment if he didn't desist – and entrusted the couple's two little boys to the care of a motherly neighbour. In the morning, when the couple had had time to sober down and George called on them, they expressed due gratitude for his irregular but effective ministrations.

It was while he was in Bermondsey that George first had a chance of exercising that compassionate ministry among boys which was to be such a feature of his Peckham period – the parish owning a club-room that was used by the local lads. His compassion towards the under-privileged was of course grounded in his memories of the hardships of his own childhood. But it had another particular cause. Brother Patrick, SSF, recalls being told that it arose in part from the fact that, as an adolescent, George had himself been ill-used by a man under whose influence he had fallen, and that this had been the turning-point in his life and a root cause of his fellow-feeling for others.

*　　*　　*

A turning-point of even greater significance came in 1923, when Burge's successor as Bishop of Southwark, Cyril Garbett, asked George to accept the living of St Chrysostom, Peckham. The future Archbishop of York minced no words when he made the offer. The parish was, he said, the most derelict in the diocese. When George went on a visit of inspection he found, like the Queen of Sheba in reverse, that the half had not been told him. The churchyard was a rubbish-dump, and the church had so many holes in its roof that a flotilla of buckets and baths had to be stationed all over the building to catch the incoming rain-water. The clock in the turret had long ago ceased to function,

as had the antiquated stove in the crypt which was the only
source of heating. The crypt itself was filled with decayed
flowers and wreaths, the detritus of past funerals. The altar,
covered by a brown army blanket for frontal, supported a cross
and a pair of brass candlesticks green with mould.

The retiring vicar was a sick man who had long ago lost
heart. He lived in a smart house outside the parish, bequeathed
George a debit balance of seventeen pounds and warned him to
keep a sharp look-out at baptisms; at his last one, he said, he had
been hit in the eye by a pea from a boy's catapult. Nothing
daunted ('I feel that God spoke to me there'), George wrote to
Garbett to accept the challenge. But, in the absence of a vicarage,
he decided to pitch his camp in the ancient parish hall. He
moved in a week or so before his induction, together with three
homeless boys whom he had decided to befriend. He was
instituted and inducted to the cure of souls at St Chrysostom's
on 8 October 1923. The church was crowded for the occasion
with friends from Wimbledon and Bermondsey as well as locals.
Garbett in later year remembered a small boy calling to the
people round the door, 'Make way for the old gentleman'
(meaning himself). He and George were apprehensive lest the
rickety galleries round the church might fail to bear the weight
of such an unaccustomed overflow of churchgoers, but all was
well. Garbett preached from a text from Joshua, 'Be strong and
of a good courage'. It was an entirely suitable exhortation in the
circumstances. The Bishop obviously thought highly of George's
potential and, when he heard what was planned, assured him:
'Do as you wish; I trust you!'

George felt that the church services needed to be enriched
with colour and ceremonial if congregations were ever to be
attracted (his first service in Peckham had been attended by
three adults and two children), so he instituted a parish Eucharist
at 9.30am with vestments and incense. But it was his own
charismatic personality as well as the ceremonial he introduced
that soon began to attract the crowds.

What was it about St Chrysostom's that made it so different
from other churches in the neighbourhood? Supremely it was
George's ability to make church-attendance a pleasure as well as

a duty. He had an abiding sense of fun – a lasting memory of 'St Chryssie's' was of hearing an entire congregation actually *laughing* in church. One former worshipper found herself attracted by the 'glorious informality coupled with the deepest reverence' of the parish Mass. The service lasted exactly an hour and was followed by a parish breakfast – which allowed those who had a stall in the Sunday market in the High Street time for a bite to eat before opening up their stalls. This was a real boon in days when service-times were rigidly restricted to 8 and 11am at other churches in the neighbourhood.

George was keen on Scouting, which he regarded as a serious activity never to be undertaken lightly. Any Scout, for instance, wishing to be made a Rover had to keep a Saturday-night vigil in the church, with his equipment on the altar, before being invested before the congregation at Mass the following morning. There was a monthly Church Parade for the uniformed organizations. On these occasions George would push the Cubs closer together and stand on the end of their pew to preach. A former Guide recalls:

> He put one foot up on the back of the pew, tucked his thumbs into his girdle and started, 'Now just to fix our attention for this morning . . .'; and, while I listened fascinated to a short sermon full of pithy points, I also held my breath in terror as he swayed back and forth, for fear that he would dive head-first into the Cubs, almost literally under his feet.

His sermons were always short and to the point. They usually began with a personal anecdote to which the congregation could easily relate – e.g., he might begin 'As I was walking down past the market stalls in Rye Lane last week . . .' He soon instituted a daily Mass (except for one day-off weekly) – and never once in his fifteen years as vicar was he left at the altar alone. 'On my first Sunday I asked people to promise to be there, three each day, and in the early days I must admit that the server slept in the hall – sometimes in the vestry.'

There was of course a lot that needed doing to the fabric of the church; but George had no difficulty in attracting volunteers to do it. Early in 1924 he formed a 'Guild of the Carpenter' for all men in the parish who could handle tools; and Guild members spent many profitable hours filling in all those holes in the roof, repainting the church both inside and out, and performing a hundred and one other necessary jobs. The Carpenters' Guild was complemented by a 'Guild of Service' to which anyone could belong. Members were responsible for a wide assortment of duties which included washing linen, teaching in the Sunday school, reading to the blind, visiting the old and lonely, cooking for the sick and performing the last offices for the dead. Not all the changes that George introduced (especially those concerned with ceremonial) were accepted automatically, but he held regular meetings at which he explained the reasons for them and soon disarmed the critics and any who were apprehensive about the new look of things. Before long the Catholic practices he introduced into St Chrysostom's were accepted without demur by almost everyone, and the size of the congregations increased by leaps and bounds.

Meanwhile he had to find a new 'vicarage', as rats were invading the parish hall from a factory next-door. They ate the food, ruined articles of clothing and had a tiresome habit of scrabbling among the potatoes during the night. The problem was solved when George discovered a derelict public house called the 'Eagle' which he persuaded the brewery which owned it to let to him for a nominal rent. The bar was turned into a combined office, lounge and bedroom for the vicar; while a notice in the window, 'This Establishment under entirely new management', appealed to the parish's sense of the ridiculous. The move to the 'Eagle', however, resulted in one early tragedy – the death of George's mother, then an old lady of nearly eighty. He had had to leave her alone while answering a sick call; and, not noticing that the cellar flap was open, she had fallen down the steps into the cellar. George returned to find her with both legs broken and her body severely bruised.

> Being the mother I knew, she merely smiled and said 'I only came to bring you a cup of tea'. She died soon afterwards. Those words always symbolise her life in my memory. She died doing a simple act of kindness, such as she had done all her life through.

*   *   *

Up till now we have seen George Potter as a thoroughly competent and inspirational parish priest, but as nothing more. But now he was to make his great decision to found a religious community to help him in his task. What led him to take so momentous a step? He recounts the origins of the Brotherhood of the Holy Cross in his autobiography. He had not been in Peckham long, he says, before he realized what a great help it would be if he could persuade a few laymen to join him, 'ready to work hard and pray hard, content to share my life, my home and my stipend'. He wanted not so much pious young men as 'the type of man who makes a good scoutmaster' (he was by then Assistant Commissioner for Rover Scouts). Then, while on retreat at Kelham, he met a man who complained that he felt lonely and to whom George revealed his vision of a fledgling community. The man was John Walton, who was at that time acting as a handyman to an order of nuns at Whitby; and, as Brother John, he was the first to join the BHC and for years acted as George's valued right-hand. Another early recruit was Brother Francis (Frank Burgess Williams), who had at one time contemplated joining Fr William Sirr at Glasshampton but had been put off by the slowness of William's recitation of the offices and by his extreme socialist views. Later he had worked as lay reader and general factotum at St Bartholomew's, Bermondsey, where he had first come across George Potter. He was to outlive George and succeed him as Father-Guardian.

These three were joined at intervals by a succession of novices, some of whom stayed for several years but others for only a few weeks or months. The community was never more than nine or ten strong even in its heyday in the 1930s, but this was due to a number of different factors which combined to deter potential recruits.

In the first place, service to people always took precedence over the ordered round of prayer to be found in a traditional religious community. Daily worship was restricted at first to Mass, Mattins, Evensong and Compline. As George put it, 'I must admit that work came first. There was so much to do'. (Of this 'work' more anon.) Indeed George himself never conformed to the generally accepted notion of a 'religious', being neither orthodox nor traditional. The 'system' was for him always secondary to people, and he never hesitated to cut through tradition and what other people considered seemly. As the *Church Times* put it on one occasion: 'Fr George never believes that holiness necessarily needs rigidity of rules as a prop. That is one of the reasons why his Community has never grown very large – for the demands on its members are as regardless of respite as are those of the gospel'. (George expressed pleasure at this pronouncement.)

Such short-circuiting of the normal monastic conventions would obviously offend many would-be recruits, though George never hesitated to turn away those whom he considered unsuitable. He put his cards bluntly on the table in an article he wrote for the *BHC Quarterly* during 1932. The Brotherhood, he said, could offer little time for quietness or contemplation. It needed men who had a very real vision of Christ and could feel near him in work and noise as well as in the peace of the sanctuary. 'No man would be happy here if he can only find Christ at Mass. At least two days a week he will be busy with porridge, blacking and vim while the others are at Mass.' Nor must a man sulk 'if he cannot get to Vespers on the Feast of St Thermogene' – he might be sitting in a police-court waiting for a 'client'. George went on:

> He mustn't be the type who goes into the kitchen and sobs just because we run short of incense. . . . We don't want men who hope to find a back door to the priesthood. They will probably add to their vocabulary considerably, but it will be neither Greek nor Latin. . . . We put prayer and sacraments first. We know we cannot do our best otherwise. But the fact is that we have to spend more time at the bottom of the Mount of Transfiguration than at the top.

George put it even more pithily on another occasion when he remarked that he couldn't see much sense in sitting on one's behind all day saying the 119th psalm when so much needed to be done with and for people. He had no use for the type of

would-be friar who was quite happy when swinging a censer at
Mass but less happy when preparing breakfast for a crowd of
noisy boys. There was little at the BHC to attract men who
could only find Jesus Christ at the altar – no salary, little peace
or comfort, and lots of work. Once an aspirant from a public
school arrived and was asked to help bath the boys and clean the
bathrooms. 'I didn't come to do that', he complained. 'I came to
live the religious life'. He was at once sent packing. As George
summed it up: 'His life of devoted service to the Blessed Master
lasted about seven minutes'. It is hardly surprising that novices
should have come and gone with considerable frequency.

George himself felt highly flattered when one young postulant
remarked of him: 'You see, Fr Potter has such a Church of
England outlook!' The Brothers wore a dark-grey double-
breasted cassock with the Franciscan knotted cord for a girdle,
from which was suspended a small cross. George always considered habits to be of secondary importance, though he admitted
that 'they do stand for something definite with men and women
who have given their whole lives to Christ in a particular
religious community; and I feel there should be some distinction
between such and others who can only go part of the way'.
George himself often appeared in various forms of ecclesiastical
undress – sometimes a rope, sometimes a belt; sometimes a
hooded scapular, sometimes not. He once shocked Patrick by
marching through the streets of Nunhead in a 'perfectly awful
leather jerkin over his habit'.*

He was often telling stories of the extraordinary young men
whom he met in the course of his ministry. 'One, I remember,
looked so very important, even prelatical, that I wondered
whether I ought to have genuflected and kissed the ring he
wore, but another server told me he was a shop assistant during
the day. One who stayed [at the friary] wore a crucifix fifteen
inches long. He took it off when I suggested he might prefer
one *we* had that was nearly four feet long.'

---

*George took his revenge on Patrick when the latter arrived for a quiet day at the
friary wearing a habit with no fewer than 106 patches. George, for once 'correctly'
garbed, remarked with quick wit: 'Brother Quilt, I presume?'

The formal objectives of the BHC were set out regularly in the *Quarterly*. The Brotherhood, they said,

> consists of men working together under the patronage of St Francis of Assisi, and with the approval of the Lord Bishop of Southwark, bound by a simple rule. Their aim is to gather together those whose vocation proves to be such as does not demand the greater detachment required by most Religious communities, and to express the Love of the Living Christ by humble service to their fellow-men.

The statement of aims was reinforced by a Book of Principles which explained the Brotherhood's rule in greater detail, set out the various duties to be performed, and expounded the three counsels of poverty, chastity and obedience.

From the start the BHC enjoyed the warm support of the Bishop of Southwark, its official Visitor. But Garbett was against its attempting to rush its fences. He considered that there should be a long period of probation before the first professions were made; and it was in fact his successor, George Parsons (afterwards Bishop of Hereford), who in June 1933 heard the professions of both George and John – eight years after the Brotherhood had been born. The novices took simple vows, and George was installed as Superior. The community had now officially 'arrived': it was a recognized religious community of the Church of England, and George could justifiably refer to 'our great day'.

As the years went by the original simple sequence of Mass, Mattins, Evensong and Compline gave way to a more elaborate liturgical routine. But even then not everyone was expected to attend every office: the demands of ministry continued to take precedence. The day began with Prime at 6.30, followed by Mattins and Mass. Breakfast was at 7.30, and at 8 a start was made on the household chores. Terce at 8.40 was followed by the morning meditation, after which the Brothers dispersed to their various tasks in house, office or garden. They reassembled for Sext at 12.45pm and lunch at 1pm. After None at 2pm work continued until tea at 4pm. Then came a short period of recreation, followed by Evensong at 5.40 and supper at 6.30. After supper there was a period set aside for reading and study. The day closed with Compline at 9.30pm; and by 10.30 most of the Brothers had retired to bed. Set out like this the routine may sound over-tidy, but of course there were constant emergencies to interrupt it. And the very nature of the duties the Brothers performed meant that the life they lived was anything but quiet.

In *Father Potter of Peckham* George gives a graphic illustration of those duties by quoting the remarks made by a succession of callers at their gate. A policeman brought along a lad whom he had found wandering about but whom he didn't want to charge ('Will you take him in?'). A probation officer arrived with another lad discharged after his first offence ('I know the magistrate would like him to come here'). A priest came to ask if a young server who seemed to be going to pieces could stay with the Brothers for a month or so. A small child in tears blurted out: 'Pussy's ill! Will you put her away?' A parishioner called to ask if a Brother could go and lay out a neighbour who had just died. A church worker asked if a Brother could go and mind a sick child to give the mother a respite. A verger wondered whether any of the Brothers could take Evensong for his vicar ('He has to be away'). And a wife came round to say: 'My old man's drunk. He's locked himself in his room and he's got his razor out!' George comments proudly: 'We said "Yes!" to all these'.

It was for his work among boys, especially delinquent boys, that he will best be remembered. They were undoubtedly his first love − and at times became a source of friction within the community as some of the Brothers felt that George's obsession with this particular side of the work prevented the BHC from developing into a proper religious order. His concern for boys had begun in his South Wimbledon days, when, as a young curate, he had been asked by a distracted mother to come and discipline her unruly son. In the end the lad was taken to court and sent to a reformatory, but the incident left George with a feeling that a system which could allow a boy to be carted off in this fashion was wrong. 'All the boy needed was some affection and discipline. It was then I decided that I wanted to have a home for youngsters like him.'

This side of George's work had begun on an *ad hoc* basis. To begin with he had shared the parish hall with three homeless youngsters. When he moved to the 'Eagle' he was able to take in a few more. But there was obvious room for expansion, so he was overjoyed when the diocesan authorities came to the rescue and purchased a house in Hill Street, Peckham, for conversion into a permanent new vicarage. Together with his two sisters, now among his most devoted helpers,* George took possession in December 1927 – leaving Brother John to adapt the old 'Eagle' for use as a club-room, conference centre and Scout headquarters. In moving into the vicarage George was allowing his role as Vicar of St Chrysostom's to take precedence over his headship of the BHC; and this too was a subsequent cause of friction, as the Brothers' enforced separation from their Superior was far from ideal. It meant that the BHC was in danger of becoming a collection of individuals rather than a community, its members being left to shape their own lives and go their own way instead of all being assembled together under the one roof. The parish at this stage came before the friary in George's order of priorities. The situation was eased to some extent in 1938, when, following a severe attack of gastritis, he was persuaded to give up the charge of the parish and go to live at the friary instead. But he was absent so often on missions to other parishes and on prison visiting that things in the end were much the same as before.

But this is to anticipate. Two years after moving into the new vicarage George felt the need for further expansion. The parish owned a disused and antiquated shirt-and-pyjama factory in Peckham High Street, and this was converted into a new headquarters for the BHC. One large room became the sleeping quarters for fourteen homeless boys, and another was divided into six cubicles for the Brothers. The former coal-cellar housed the bathroom and laundry, and a cottage attached to the building provided a sick-room, kitchen and office. A friendly builder

---

*They moved later to take charge of a house at Southwick, Sussex, which was given to the BHC by a well-wisher and converted into a holiday home for the parish. The sisters ran the home till their deaths in 1947 and 1948.

carried out the necessary structural changes; and a well-wisher
who was going abroad presented a vast amount of her redundant
furniture to the renamed 'Hostel of St Francis'.

The boys themselves represented a variety of backgrounds.
Some were orphans; some came from overcrowded homes or
were dumped on the Brothers because their parents were unable
to cope with them. The authorities became interested in this side
of the BHC's work, and sent round first offenders or other lads
in need of care and protection. George comments wryly: 'In
most cases the real cause of the trouble for the boys was their
parents'. In his autobiography he recalls that, out of nearly nine
hundred boys who had come into the care of the Brotherhood
over a thirty-year period, only twenty-two had had good, normal
homes. 'So many children start life with the handicap of a bad
home, a lack of love and understanding and sane discipline, with
a spot of vice added often enough. We have had boys who were
slaves at home, and others who were taught to steal.' Most of
the latter had been guilty of petty larceny, though the more
intelligent ones might have forged cheques or stolen motor-cars.
'Many of these crimes have needed brains and courage.' George
tells many moving anecdotes about his charges and speaks of the
deep affection many of them came to feel for the Brothers (and
which was fully reciprocated). He quotes an extract from an
article in the *BHC Quarterly* in which an 'old boy' who had been
referred to the BHC by the magistrates records his impressions
of the hostel:

> Fr George Potter came for me. He looked so big and strong, but
> he had a kind face, so I wasn't really frightened. On the way
> home on a 'bus he said to me, 'What you want is a jolly good
> hiding!' I looked at him and shuddered. . . . For a week I tried all
> sorts of pranks. I was a devil. But they were so kind I suppose I
> saw sense. But don't think there ain't no discipline. . . . Fr George
> can lay it on pretty thick at times. . . . What I like too is that they
> [the Brothers] *ask* you to do things and don't shout at you.

Success bred success; and the Brotherhood's reputation in the
field of delinquent-boy-care was such that in 1931 it was asked
by the chairman of the local juvenile court to run another home

for boys on probation. He told George that a fellow-magistrate, H.L. Cancellor, had founded a hostel for boys at Basingstoke in Hampshire but was no longer able to carry it on. Could the Brothers take over the hostel and relaunch it in their own part of London? By chance George called that evening at the local Boot's library and noticed among the volumes on the shelves a book by Cancellor, *The Life of a London Beak*, in the course of which he told the story of how he had come to found his hostel. George considered the coincidence divinely-inspired and agreed to take it on. A suitable property was found in Peckham Rye, renamed Cancellor House, and blessed by Bishop Garbett. It provided accommodation for twenty-two boys, but soon the space available proved insufficient; and, with the help of Cancellor's widow Lily, a much larger house with over two acres of garden was purchased in Linden Grove, Nunhead. This was big enough to house forty boys and ten Brothers. They sold the original Cancellor House and moved into their new headquarters in 1934; an old stable was made into a chapel.

The new friary was a typical mid-Victorian brick building on three floors, with a porch resting on stucco columns; it was set well back from a quiet road. The rooms were shabby but homely, and were furnished with an assortment of unmatching items bequeathed to the Brothers by well-wishers who had no further use for them. The garden seemed an oasis of peace in the busy hive of London. Trees and flower-beds abounded; the fruit and vegetables grown by the Brothers helped feed them and their young charges.

There was now plenty of room for the Brothers and the boys; though, when he compared the new abode with the rat-ridden parish hall, the derelict pub, the converted factory and the mark-one Cancellor House, George often found himself hankering after the 'warmer, romantic simplicity of those pioneer days'. Nor did he have any illusions about the basic flaws in human nature. He quotes from a poem written by a brother priest about a superior requesting entrance to Heaven:

> 'What have you done,' St Peter said,
> 'That you seek admission here?'

'I ran a Delinquents' Home on earth
For many and many a year'.
St Peter opened wide the gate,
And gently pressed the bell.
'Come in', he said, 'and choose your harp;
You've *had* your share of hell!'

In spite of the frequency with which recruits to the Brotherhood came and went it continued to grow, and by the early 'thirties consisted of the Superior, three other Brothers and five novices. In 1932 Brother John was appointed Prior; he supervised the work of the community and trained the novices and postulants, leaving George free to concentrate on the work of the parish. But, as Superior, the latter still had many BHC duties which he was unable to delegate; and the strain of the double burden, coupled with recurring attacks of gastritis, was such that he was obliged in 1937 to take a prolonged rest. For some years the BHC had enjoyed close links with the Brotherhood of St Francis of Assisi, which was to merge with the Brotherhood of the Love of Christ to form the Society of St Francis; and it was the SSF which now came to the rescue. It sent Fr Denis Marsh to take charge of the parish for a year. But, at the end of that year, George was still not sufficiently recovered to resume his dual role, so, on the advice both of his doctor and of Bishop Parsons, he surrendered the care of the parish permanently. Fr Francis, SSF (William Tyndale-Biscoe), was appointed Vicar of St Chrysostom's in 1938, with George as his honorary curate. But he still celebrated and preached there often, so his curacy proved far from nominal; and it was hardly surprising that he should have collapsed again on Christmas Eve, 1938. He underwent an operation in 1939 which, for the time being, restored him to health.

This was just as well, for, with the outbreak of war in 1939 and the onset of the German blitz the following year, conditions in the parish, as in the rest of London, became horrendous; and, if George had been out of action for long periods of time, the remaining Brothers would have found it hard to cope. As it was, he really came into his own. Peckham was in the borough of

Camberwell, which suffered badly from the bombing. By the
end of the war only eight places of worship within a one-mile
radius of the friary, out of twenty-six standing in 1939, were fit
to be used. Over twenty incendiaries fell in the immediate
neighbourhood, and on two occasions the friary caught fire.
Two high explosives hit the garden, one leaving a crater thirty
feet in diameter. Windows and doors were blown out many
times, and an entire street was wrecked within two hundred
yards of the house.

The number of boys being looked after by the Brothers fell
during the war from forty-six to twenty-two. Many bombed-out
folk found shelter at the friary, some of them staying for
months. Two elderly sisters slept in a brush-cupboard and
another old lady in the larder; others slept on the floor of the
cellar. In the garden were eight Anderson shelters, each accommo-
dating six boys and an adult. George himself always slept in the
chapel; he insisted on donning his pyjamas every night, even
though it might be for only a few minutes before the first air-
raid alert. Many of the friary's 'old boys' joined the Forces,
some gaining commissions and three being awarded decorations
for bravery. They would send cheery letters to George. One
wrote: 'I've never prayed so much in my life, but I've done a lot
in the past six weeks. You taught me how to do it, and I'm
grateful'.

The war years undoubtedly marked the high-spot of George's
ministry in Peckham. A memorable picture of his unflappability
at that time has been left by Brother Patrick, SSF. Whenever he
thinks of George Potter, he told Brother John Charles,

> the picture which comes most clearly to my mind is of him seated
> in a deep armchair surrounded by about a dozen boys: calm,
> placid, smilingly telling the most unlikely stories and holding
> eveyone's attention – and this during one of London's heaviest
> bombing raids during the war. Outside, absolute inferno; inside,
> despite the noise, there radiated a calm which sustained both the
> visiting probation officer and myself. *We* were terrified, but to
> George and the boys it seemed 'old hat'.

After the war the Brotherhood resumed its normal activities and took on others, but there was now a subtle difference in the main 'clientèle' – the boys themselves. George put his finger on this in a comment he made in the *BHC Quarterly* for Easter 1953. He felt, he said, that the lad of today was different from the lad of thirty years ago, in that there was no moral background on which to build character. There was something missing in their make-up.

> We have had some real tough-guys in the past – thieves, forgers, gangsters, fathers at 15 years, etc., but I found one could nearly always get down to some sense of penitence, guilt and shame in them. It is not so today. Why? Largely, I think, because, having no religion, they have no moral sense. Home life means so little, too, and, the cinema being their chief means of entertainment and education since leaving school, the background of life has become so unreal . . .

That, of course, was written before television had made much impact on society. George's comments today would no doubt have been far harsher.

In other respects, too, he tended to look back with nostalgia to the pre-Welfare State days, when there had been so much more for the Brothers to do in the way of practical works of mercy – 'when we were surrounded by really poor folks and when the Brothers could help by nursing the sick and performing the Last Offices for the Dead; by cooking and cleaning up for the old and bedridden, stripping and painting dirty, verminous walls and the like'. He continued:

> Now there is no opportunity for that. The Welfare State and high wages have changed all that, and personally I find it difficult to adjust myself to the new routine. . . . I suppose the Founder of a Community is bound to feel the strain of a change of policy in the course of development. How our dear St Francis suffered in that way!

The changed conditions under the Welfare State led George to throw himself more and more into outside activities – in particular, parish missions and work among prisoners.

He considered that missions were the best way to evangelise
Britain and that they presented a splendid opportunity for
members of religious orders. He began the planning for each
mission about two years in advance. He would pay a preliminary
visit to his chosen parish on an ordinary Sunday to explain his
strategy. Then, six months later, he would meet as many committed churchgoers as possible in the parish hall to persuade them
to undertake a full-scale visitation of the parish and to give them
some hints on visiting techniques. Each visitor would be encouraged to call on ten families in the parish, and a report on each
visit would be submitted to the incumbent. Each family who
admitted to being 'C of E' would then be visited again several
times over the course of the next eighteen months or so. During
the actual week or ten days of the mission George would
celebrate daily and also conduct a service every evening in
church at which he would give two short addresses: one as part
of a course of instruction, the other as a more devotional
homily. He would also answer any questions sent in during the
week, be in church for an hour or so each morning and evening
to hear confessions and give private counsel, and visit sick
parishioners unable to get to church.

He often took meals at various houses in the parish, though,
as he ruefully remarked, 'a ten-day mission means forty meals,
and most of the dear folk make one very welcome indeed!' On
one occasion he stepped on to a pair of bathroom scales at the
end of the mission and found he had put on three stone in
weight. It was just as well that, since his operation, he had no
longer suffered from gastritis. Sometimes he held meetings in
pubs – 'I usually find that the publicans are very ready to help
and are courteous enough to come along to church'.

Prison visiting was the other of George's main extra-parochial
activities in the post-war years. His work among prisoners dated
back to 1919, when he addressed two hundred old lags at Camp
Hill, next-door to Parkhurst Prison on the Isle of Wight. On that
occasion the congregation, to begin with, would neither sing nor
pray nor show any interest whatever in the proceedings, so he was
reduced to desperate measures to wake them up. Despite the
advice of the chaplain not to 'talk about sin', he began his sermon:

> I come from Bermondsey. For a whole year we've been working
> hard in preparing for a sale of work. Last Saturday we made £78,
> and during the night two gentlemen of one of the oldest profes-
> sions in the world got through a window and pinched the lot!

That not only woke the congregation up but aroused their
sympathy. There were gasps all round. Later, when George
visited the inmates in their cells, one of them assured him: 'No
decent burglar would have done that, sir!' Another commented:
'I call that a . . . shame, gov'nor!'

George gradually extended his prison visiting, and became a
firm favourite with the governors and warders as well as with
many of the prisoners themselves. Once, in a crowded bus, a
man exclaimed (to George's acute embarrassment): 'Scuse me,
Father. Weren't you in Wandsworth Jail with me last year?'
Sometimes George conducted a ten-day mission within a prison,
which gave him time for a definite course of instruction as well
as for dozens of cell visits. But, as he remarks in his autobiography, 'even in ten days there is precious little time to meet all
those who make application for a visit. I can do only eight or
ten a day. An hour is not long to spend with a man who wants
to tell his life story, and also to discuss spiritual problems'. Once
he met an ex-prisoner who had been discharged after a life
sentence and whose son he had taken into the friary fifteen years
before.

> I had heard the man condemned to death, and later reprieved, and
> I had visited him about twice a year for twelve years. On the day
> of discharge I met him at the gate of the prison. He was a very
> lonely man, tearful and bewildered. He came home with me and
> stayed for a year or so. . . . [On the day after his arrival] I sent
> him for a walk round Peckham Rye, but he came back trembling.
> He was used to being watched wherever he went, and the traffic
> and crowds frightened him. It took him days to get used to
> knives and forks, and he would sit and mutter to himself.

A religious preaching in a prison chapel always starts with an
advantage over a secular priest, for his habit and vows speak
clearly of sacrifice and commitment, virtues much admired by

prisoners. George's strong face, his record of work among disadvantaged and delinquent boys, his understanding of the prisoners' own culture, his fund of good stories and his ready wit all helped him to establish a ready *rapport* with his listeners. Bishop Leslie Lloyd Rees, a former Chaplain-General of Prisons, recalls a visit paid by George to Dartmoor in 1949, and of his being given a set of keys by the Governor to enable him to visit the men in their cells. 'One place which attracted him like a magnet was E wing, the segregation unit which housed men convicted of offences against prison discipline and where his ability to listen patiently to grievances and feelings of injustice, imagined or otherwise, did much to defuse explosive situations. As one rebellious man commented: "Father George helped me because he was a bit of a rebel himself".'

As a result of George's visits to Dartmoor several of the prisoners asked to be allowed to stay at the friary after their release. Many did so – and discovered that life there was almost as tough and demanding as it had been in prison! Ex-prisoners who called only in the expectation of using George and even of manipulating him soon discovered that he was no easy touch and could often anticipate their next move before they made it. One old friend from Dartmoor, however, was accepted as a postulant and eventually became a novice. Bishop Lloyd Rees records the remark of a rather bewildered prisoner who said of George: 'He's either a first-class con man or a saint, and I'm not sure which!'

While George busied himself on missions to parishes and prisons he was also concerned to maintain the outreach of the Brotherhood itself, which expanded in a number of directions in the post-war years.

Just before Christmas 1949 Brother Francis, who had been with the BHC almost from the start, went with Brother Laurence to take charge of a mission church in the parish of Holy Trinity, Waltham Cross, at the request of its vicar, Jack Catterick. This gave Francis a chance to test his vocation to the priesthood, though George was to miss him sorely – 'he had a way of doing little acts of love that a tired "old man" appreciates'. By now there was a very mixed crowd living hugger-mugger at the friary in Linden Grove, students (theological, medical and musical) having joined the Brothers and working lads since the war. The friary was at No. 66. Next-door, at No. 64, Brother Peter and a lay helper were in charge of fifteen younger boys at the Holy Cross Hostel. Another boys' hostel was opened in 1947 at Stanford-le-Hope, Essex, in the house previously occupied by the Society of the Divine Compassion; the following year it moved to the war-damaged Holy Trinity Vicarage at Lee, in south-east London. The Brotherhood even expanded out of the Home Counties when Brother Bernard opened a community house for coloured folk in Manchester. By mid-1955 it had five different spheres of work – the friary itself; the Holy Cross Hostel; the hostel at Lee; the Waltham Cross mission; and the house at Manchester – 'and only nine of us to share the work'. It was a lot to manage, and George admitted as much when he remarked about this time that the community life suffered from the dispersal of the BHC's members in a host of outside activities. 'I have to admit, also, that my aims and ideals and plan of life were practical thirty years ago, but are not likely to satisfy the average young man who wants a Community Life today – unless he has the rather unconventional outlook on life and service as is mine. We must do justice to the younger members who come to join us and aim at a more regular life.'

It was in order to help get a 'more regular life' going at the friary that the Society of St Francis, with which the BHC still enjoyed close links, again lent them Fr Denis, who had taken charge of St Chrysostom's for a year in 1937–38 but who was in 1955 seconded to the BHC as its 'Warden'. George himself became 'Father-Guardian' rather than 'Superior'.

* * *

Towards the end of his life George was persuaded to tell the story of that life and of the community he had founded to a wider public. The result was *Father Potter of Peckham*, published in 1955. Much of the book is autobiographical. It is written in a racy style and with an artless simplicity that at once endears the writer to his audience. Its sequel, *More Father Potter of Peckham*, is less successful; it bears all the hallmarks of a book written to the order of a publisher anxious to exploit a best-selling author. There is less about George himself and more about the community; but there are some good anecdotes, and no doubt *More Father Potter* pleased his admirers. Both books are embellished with delightful line-drawings to complement the text. Some of the material in both had already appeared in print: in the *BHC Quarterly*, a lively magazine in which the growth and development of the community can be traced from its early days until its demise after George's death. He sometimes appeared on TV during the 1950s. On one occasion, after he had put his beloved pipe on the table, he received an indignant letter lecturing him on the 'evils of smoking' (this of course was in the days before the connection with lung cancer had been established). Following another appearance he was annoyed to receive letters from Roman Catholic viewers anxious to persuade him to join the 'true Church'.

His hard-spent life was now drawing to its close. On 5 June 1959 he suffered a coronary thrombosis (following an attack of diabetes) and was rushed by ambulance to Dulwich Hospital. He philosophically regarded his enforced idleness as a salutary lesson, quoting the words of Wilson Carlile: 'The Lord put me on my back in order that I might look up'. In an article appearing in the *BHC Quarterly* in September he remarked that he thought God must have had a word with his guardian angel and told him to make George rest for a few weeks.

> I thank God for what happened. It has taught me so much. God decided that I had to realize that I am 72 years of age and not 27, so He warned me by letting my heart fail to function. The fact that two Brothers were with me at the time and my doctor available, and that a bed was found for me at this hospital – within a mile of the Friary – tells me that He still wants me to carry on – at a slower pace – for a few years yet. I am really thankful.

He was in and out of hospital for the next five months, and, during his spells back at the friary, settled down to a routine of praying, reading and letter-writing, quite content to wait on God's will for the future. He was even able to conduct a few

services at the local crematorium. On the day before he died he
had preached in the chapel of Dulwich College and was his old,
cheery self. So he remained on 'active service' to the last.

He died on 15 February 1960 after receiving the Blessed
Sacrament from Stanley Ashby, Vicar of St Antholin's (later
renamed St Antony's), Nunhead.* The funeral took place on 20
February in St Chrysostom's, which was packed to the doors.
The requiem was sung by the Bishop of Southwark, Mervyn
Stockwood, the tone of the whole service being one of thanksgiving and rejoicing. The church was bedecked with flowers; and
the singing was joyful and unrestrained. The spirit of joy and
thanksgiving was maintained in the 'oration' by Stockwood's
predecessor, Bertram Simpson, who gave a vivid account of
George's life and ministry. The requiem was followed immediately by the funeral office, after which the body was borne to
Honor Oak Crematorium, where Fr Francis said the words of
committal and final prayers.

After George's death the chapel at the friary was restored and
reconstructed in his memory. Hanging on its west wall was the
portrait of George by Delmar Banner which had been exhibited
at the Royal Academy in 1959. There is also a memorial to him
in Southwark Cathedral. He had been made an honorary canon
of the cathedral in 1954 in recognition of his long and devoted
service to the diocese, and there is now a stall there in his
memory. An annual festival at Holy Crosstide was instituted at
St Antony's, Nunhead.

*   *   *

'I only met Fr George once, and then very briefly, but he
impressed me as being the only true Christian I have ever met.'
This was one of many appreciations of George to be printed in
the *BHC Quarterly* after his death – chosen out of 'the hundreds

---

*This was the parish which now included the friary in Linden Grove. St Chrysos-
tom's had been restored after suffering damage in the war, and George had still
gone there once a month to sing the parish Mass. Later the foundations were found
to be unsafe and the building had to be demolished. The parish now forms part of
the new parish of St John, Peckham. Canon Ashby was Vicar of St Antony's from
1952 to 1972; he went on to be Vicar of Blackheath.

sent to us'. George had indeed made an immense impact on his own neighbourhood and far beyond. In his lifetime he was so well known that letters addressed to him simply as 'Father Potter of Peckham' (and even, on one occasion, to 'The Fat Friar of Peckham') would be safely delivered. The obituarists vied with each other in piling on the superlatives, as is the way of obituarists; and indeed this brief account of his life will have given at least some indication of the essential saintliness of his character. But even saints have, if not feet of clay, at any rate an Achilles heel. And for an objective portrait of George one must go not so much to admiring tributes in the newspapers as to the assessments by those who knew him well during his lifetime. Four such assessments were made in 1971, eleven years after his death, by three of his former colleagues (Fr Francis and Brothers Arnold and Patrick) and by Canon Ashby. They were made in response to an appeal by Brother John Charles, SSF, who was contemplating a full-scale account of the Franciscan revival in the Anglican Communion. Together they paint a warts-and-all picture of George which makes him, if anything, more endearing (and certainly more human) than the plaster-saint portraits by some of his obituarists.

The basic facet of his character was that he was a 'loner', and the basic weakness of the BHC under his rule that it was made to depend on and centre on himself. Everything was fine while he was there, but, when he was absent (as he was frequently in his later years), there was no clear direction. As a result, when he died, there was no obvious leader to succeed him. He was too much of an individualist really to hit it off with his colleagues. As a result the BHC sometimes appeared more like a collection of individuals than an integrated community.

He failed to instil the spirit of obedience in his subordinates. As Francis remarks in his assessment, 'for too long we had our own way'. In the case of the BHC there was no Algy to hold the reins when its Douglas, i.e., George, was away on one of his frequent missions. Francis thinks that this was the real reason why, in the end, George cried off from anything more than the loosest kind of association with the other Franciscan societies. His failure to agree to a closer relationship came as a great disappointment to Fr Algy at Hilfield; but Algy was keen on monastic discipline, and that kind of discipline had never appealed to George. Francis describes George as a 'very dear man but very peculiar' – not a good superior nor even a good religious. He was always out preaching, and there was no one to take his place. No foundations were securely laid. But Francis admits that George was kind, loving and lovable and 'did much for many'.

To Patrick the outstanding quality of George was his compassion for others – 'like Brother Douglas he could look into a man's eyes and see God'. He had a particular sympathy for young lads from disadvantaged backgrounds. 'He was often let down, but I don't think he ever failed anyone who had come into his care.'

George's room at the friary was never locked. There was a notice on the door: 'Please knock and enter'. He was always available at any time of the day or night and always listened to what people had to say. 'If he thought you were wasting his time or being foolish', says Arnold, 'he never left you in any doubt.' Arnold thought George a great priest whose prime consideration was for people, and a markedly 'spiritual' person (though not of a textbook type). He was a very trusting man, but was no good at exercising discipline over others. Hard work all day was George's prescription. He was not all that keen on his colleagues taking time off for study – which led to friction and tensions within the community. The boys were another source of friction, since it was felt that they took up too much of George's time. Arnold echoes the other assessors in adding plaintively: 'But the real weakness was that Potter was never *there*'.

Perhaps the most valuable of the postmortem assessments is that of Canon Ashby, who could look at George more objectively than could his former colleagues. Ashby found George a 'very attractive person', who you could always talk to and talk things over with. He was a very human man and, in Ashby's judgment, sensible in his advice and one in whom he had complete confidence. His discretion was absolute. He was a great preacher and missioner, very natural and not in the least parsonic. Towards the end of his life he grew repetitive: his stories came from the past and people had heard them before. But he was essentially, says Ashby, a *humble* man.

There are many people still living who will remember George Potter – that rather stocky figure in grey habit and sandals with his attractive smile and cheery voice. In the course of a tribute printed in the *Church Times* after his death Bishop Simpson remarked that George's wide appeal was due largely to his intense humanity, his interest in ordinary affairs, his common sense, his deep sympathy and understanding in dealing with individuals and his boundless sense of fun. 'Most powerful of all was that simple, direct devotion to our Lord which was so natural as to amount almost to personal friendship. To be in his presence was to breathe something of that atmosphere. . . . His intimate touch with the seamy side of life, and even with its degraded depths, never clouded the serenity of his faith.'

*   *   *

After George's death the Brotherhood's postscript without him was sadly brief. Even before his death Arnold had pinpointed the basic issue when he wrote in the *BHC Quarterly*: 'To maintain our present scope of works will necessitate a flow of fresh blood into the Brotherhood, a new intake of ideas, a coming to grips afresh with the kind of works a Community such as ours sets out to do in the first instance. This has been brought home more and more with the illness of Fr George and the consequent devolution of new responsibility on to the Brethren severally. . . . The smallness of the Community has made itself felt'. Echoing George's order of priorities, Arnold pointed out that they did not want 'pious young men who glow with rapture over diurnals and ordos', but neither did they want young men whose only interest was in social works. 'We do need and want men who will happily combine the worship of God in chapel with the service of God in their fellow-men.'

Alas, such men were not forthcoming; and the absence of new recruits sealed the fate of the Brotherhood. The existing Brothers now numbered a mere half-dozen or so, but they were still responsible for the work at the Nunhead friary, the Manchester community centre and the boys' hostel at Lee. In addition they had taken on new duties in the parish of St Mary, Rotherhithe; while Fr Francis, now an ordained priest, had moved from Waltham Cross to a similar sphere of work at Houghton Conquest in Bedfordshire.

The first item of business was to elect a successor to George as Father-Guardian. The obvious candidate was the second-in-command, Brother Giles (Frank Leslie Dawson), who was the only other priest normally resident at the friary. In the event, however, he was considered unsuitable for the headship of the BHC and Francis was elected to don George's mantle in spite of his isolated position in Bedfordshire. He shared the responsibility of running the Brotherhood with Giles, but there was a certain amount of internal dissension. Bishop Stockwood clearly saw that the only solution was to wind up the community, since there were not enough members to make it viable and it had no assured future before it. No outsider had really expected it to survive George's death for long, so the news of its forthcoming demise came as no real surprise.

The official announcement was given in the *BHC Quarterly* for Christmastide 1962. Francis, as Father-Guardian, pointed out that the time had come for them to face realities. 'Since Fr George's death we can see more clearly than ever before that, with all the best intentions, our work was centred around his ministry and his alone. Therefore we must do as our Visitor requests – join with the Society of St Francis in September 1963.' Francis added that, because of his age, he would be unable to take this step himself; so, with the Bishop's permission, he would stay on at Houghton Conquest as parish priest, living a simple rule of his own. Giles, who had been taken ill with a cerebral thrombosis the previous September, was among those who joined the SSF; but he never recovered his health sufficiently to be able to say Mass and died, still an invalid, on 23 October 1967, aged 60. Others to join the SSF in 1963 were Stephen (Aylward), who had been in the BHC since 1930; and Arnold (Thomas Arthur Nodder), who had joined in 1949 and had been admitted to life vows only in 1953. Stephen was renamed Nicholas, as there was already a Stephen at Hilfield; he

died in August 1983, in the fifty-fourth year of his profession.
Arnold, at the time of writing (October 1993), was living at the
Birmingham house of the SSF; he had been ordained in 1960.
Brother Bernard (Albert Bernard Ball), who had been in charge
of the BHC's Manchester centre, left the Brotherhood shortly
before his ordination in 1962 and served as a parish priest in the
diocese of Manchester, retiring in 1980.

The various buildings in which George laboured for so long
in Peckham are now all gone. The site of the friary in Linden
Grove was compulsorily acquired by the borough council for
housing development: appropriately, flats and homes for the
elderly. The friary itself was demolished. Some of the chapel
furnishings which had been made by an ex-prisoner were trans-
ferred to the crypt of St Giles's, Camberwell. But, though the
buildings are now gone and nothing material is left of George
Potter's work, much remains in lives enriched and souls saved –
and in the hearts of those who look back on him with
thanksgiving.

MAN WITH A MISSION

Brother Edward in his prime

CHAPTER 4

MAN WITH A MISSION

Brother Edward and the Village Evangelists

BISHOP WALTER CAREY once observed of his fellow-founder of the Village Evangelists: 'Brother Edward is a saint, and I am an ordinary sinner who likes his creature comforts'. And, in his autobiography, the bishop describes Edward as simply the most Christ-like man he knew. This aura of holiness struck almost everyone who came into contact with Edward — both those who knew him well and those who were meeting him for the first time. Among his associates Elizabeth Paul considered him to be very close in spirit to St Francis, while Evelyn Gedge was struck by his 'genuine, pure, humble, holy face. His face made people look and think'. This was borne out on many occasions. On one of his missions a child, opening the door to his knock, ran excitedly into the kitchen and exclaimed: 'Mummy, Jesus is on the doorstep and wants to come in!'. A young maid at a vicarage told her master: 'I did not ask his name, but I think it is the Lord Jesus has come'. One man who got into conversation with Edward on the platform of a railway station knew, by the time the train arrived, that he must change his entire way of life. Another man who gave up a business career for the priesthood through Edward's influence could hardly restrain himself from dancing for joy after hearing him preach. And a woman once wrote: 'From the moment of coming into contact with him I knew that . . . a turning-point in my life faced me and that the conventional sort of religion I had lived in was being shaken by some great force'. Edward had made up his mind while still a curate to dedicate his life unreservedly to the service of Christ and to follow as closely as he could in the footsteps of our Lord. He gave up all material possessions other than the clothes he stood up in, a bible and a crucifix. After briefly testing his vocation with the Cowley Fathers he became an itinerant missioner: tramping the roads, accepting hospitality if it was offered, but otherwise sleeping rough or in casual wards, eating berries or going without food. By the time of his death in 1953 he was known throughout the length and breadth of England as one of the greatest evangelists of the century.

*   *   *

The transition from a 'normal' life to one of total self-sacrifice was gradual. Like Fr Andrew and Brother Douglas, Edward came from a comfortable middle-class background. His paternal grandfather had kept a shop in Marylebone High Street, but his father, William Bulstrode, went into farming. He did so well that he was able to set up on his own at Mount Farm, Cookham Dean, in Berkshire. In 1858 he married Jane Taylor, whose father was agent to Lord Ebury's estate near Rickmansworth, Hertfordshire. The couple remained at Mount Farm for the first twenty-six years of their married life, the prolific Jane giving birth during this period to no fewer than thirteen children: seven sons and six daughters. Then Jane's brother Seth handed over one of his flour-mills at Wandsworth to William, who forsook farming for running what soon became a flourishing business venture. The family moved to Lancaster Lodge, Croydon, where, on 24 November 1885, William and Jane's fourteenth child, the future Brother Edward, was born. An intriguing parallel can be drawn with another outstanding evangelist, John Wesley, himself a fifteenth child.

The successful delivery of their eighth son must have come as a relief to Jane, who was in her late forties at the time of Edward's birth, had borne her last child six years earlier and was far from well during the final months of her pregnancy. She spent much of her time in bed, praying fervently during her enforced inactivity as befitted her devout Evangelical back-

ground. Edward, like Samuel in the Old Testament, was a child
of much prayer. He was baptized Edward Gordon after the hero
of Khartoum (the christening took place almost a year after the
massacre), but was always called Gordon by members of his
family. Late in 1887 the Bulstrodes moved to Down Lodge, a
large old house overlooking the Wandle Valley just outside
Wandsworth. It was here that Gordon (as we may now call him
for the time being) grew up. Both his parents were keen
churchpeople, and several of their children shared their religious
enthusiasm. Two of Gordon's brothers, Frank and Ernest, later
represented the diocese of Oxford in the House of Laity of the
Church Assembly. Two of his sisters, Jane and Emily, served as
missionaries among the Maoris of New Zealand for more than
forty years. His youngest sister, Alice, was associated with him
at various periods of his ministry. She provided a firm base to
which he could always return at times of real emergency. Among
the Bulstrodes' closest friends at Wandsworth were the Attlees.
Members of the two families joined in both church work and
social activities. The future Prime Minister recalled Gordon as a
'small boy with sleek black hair' three years his junior: in later
life they corresponded occasionally, and Gordon remembered
his illustrious contemporary every St Clement's Day, 23rd November (which happened to be the day before his own birthday).
Clement's sister Mary ran the girls' department of the Sunday
school attached to Wandsworth Parish Church, while Gordon's
brother Ernest was responsible for the boys.

As the youngest of fourteen children Gordon found himself
gradually bereft of his siblings as they quit the family nest. He
was sent first to a day school in Putney, Kingsland House, and
then (no doubt at the prompting of the Attlees, who had sent
Clement there) to Haileybury College. This was a middle-grade
public school which had been founded in 1862 and many of the
pupils of which were destined either for the Forces or for the
Civil Service. Discipline was stern and social conformity very
much *de rigueur*. Gordon, a thoughtful, independent-minded boy,
resented the constraints – preferring, for instance, to visit old
churches in the surrounding Hertfordshire countryside than to
play in school games. Such behaviour was hardly likely to make

him the most popular boy in the school. Indeed, in retrospect, he described his years at Haileybury as 'the unhappiest time of my life'. He once wrote: 'I was *so* disliked at school that it has produced that effect through my whole nature'. Nevertheless, he cannot have been as universally unpopular as he implies. He often asked his mother if he might bring a school friend home for a night or two in the holidays, and in later life kept in touch with a number of these friends (who included Sir Edwyn Hoskyns, the distinguished Biblical scholar). He was confirmed in his first year at Haileybury (21 November 1900) by the Bishop of St Albans. He said afterwards that he did not associate any special spiritual experience with the occasion; but he also revealed that it was during his time at Haileybury that he first became fully aware of his vocation to the ministry of the Church. And he spoke also of his ambition to preach in every church in England – an ambition that foreshadowed his appearance, as a roving evangelist, in innumerable pulpits up and down the land.

From Haileybury he went up in October 1904 (like Fr Andrew sixteen years earlier) to Keble College, Oxford. There, for the next four years, he lived the life of a typical undergraduate. He appears to have been far happier at college than he had been at school. He was extremely sociable, entertaining his many friends and being entertained by them. He dressed immaculately and was regarded as the 'dandy' of his year. He rowed for his college and in addition played rugger, hockey and tennis. He belonged to the college debating society and to the 'Bug-Shooters', the university branch of the Territorials. His letters to his mother throughout his time at Oxford reflect his multifarious activities and general zest for life. 'I have never been so full up before, with countless engagements, social and business meetings, etc.,' he writes to her on one occasion; and on another he enthuses about his rowing:

> The racing is absolutely glorious, though all the way you don't see how you can possibly keep on till the end ... I have never been so fit in my life as during training; it is simply grand, the feeling, though training is an awful bore. Just on the days of the

races it is almost impossible to work, and I have done awfully
little ... I am very much relishing my pipe tonight after being
denied it for so long.

Gordon's inability to work during the bumping races reflects
his easy distraction from most forms of intellectual activity. He
was no natural scholar, dreaded examinations and was bored
stiff by lectures. In the circumstances it is hardly surprising that
he should have left Oxford with a mere pass degree. In fact his
dislike of intellectual pursuits was not due to laziness or inability
to concentrate. He believed throughout his life in the prompting
of the spirit – and thought that the working of the intellect
made this more difficult to recognize and follow. On the spiritual
plane he made good use of his time at Oxford, always attending
Holy Communion in the college chapel on Sundays and afterwards going to a service at one of the city churches. He used to
report to his mother, often critically, on the sermons he had
heard. But he made no pretence to ultra-piety. His friend David
Railton, who often accompanied him on his churchgoing, later
recalled: 'He was always quite open about his religion, but in this,
as in other things, he had a sort of natural "family" way about
it. He would bounce into your room asking if you were going to
church exactly as he would ask, "Are you going to the Debate?"
He had already grasped the idea, not common among undergraduates of his time, that religion is essentially a joyous life'.

It had not always been thus. In fact Gordon's association of
faith with joy had come about through a 'conversion experience'
while at the university. He had gone one day to the Albert Hall
in London to listen to the American evangelists Torrey and
Alexander. A man at the meeting had asked him, 'Sir, are you
saved?'; and Gordon, in a holier-than-thou fit of pique, had
replied loftily, 'Thank you, sir, I've been baptized'. Afterwards,
however, he had regretted his hasty retort. 'I hadn't got the kind
of joy Christ spoke about, and I hadn't got the peace of God in
my heart ... I began to think of all the sins I had done since I
was baptized as a baby – and I saw what hypocrisy my answer
had been.' A two-part sequel to the Albert Hall meeting took
place after Gordon's return to Oxford. First, during a service in

Holy Week, 'God spoke to me and showed me that what I needed was to face out my past life more thoroughly than I had ever done before, to examine my life, and then to bring it all out in the open to my Saviour'. Secondly, on Easter Eve, having made a list of all his sins from his early days ('Very ugly it looked in black and white'), he went into church, knelt down, and told God everything – 'the things I was most ashamed of' – in the presence of a priest. 'I got up from my knees a different man. The burden of a lifetime had gone; joy and peace had become real, and the whole world had become a different place ... Afterwards came a great longing that other people might know what Jesus Christ can do for a sinner.' So, to the seeds of his first confession, can be traced the growth of Gordon's desire to become an evangelist.

During his time at the university he had also developed a social conscience. In his first year, fired by a powerful sermon against intemperance preached in the university church by the Bishop of London, A.F. Winnington-Ingram, he protested against the bizarre ceremony of the 'Freshers' Wine', which that year had sparked off a great deal of drunkenness and rowdyism. With the help of his friend Railton he succeeded in getting the 'Wine' abolished. He was always sympathizing with those in real trouble. 'We must *do* something about it', he would tell his Keble friends. He was remembered long afterwards for his championship of the under-dog – in this case the kitchen-maid – during a college debate on 'The Servant Problem'. His desire for practical Christian service soon found an outlet at the Oxford House in Bethnal Green – of which, as we have seen in the chapter on Fr Andrew – Winnington-Ingram had been a notable head. Gordon visited the House during his university vacations and helped entertain youngsters from the East End on their annual outings to Oxford. From September 1907 to March 1908, while still nominally reading for his degree, he worked full-time at the House, playing a full part in the work of the clubs and the outdoor 'slumming'. On one occasion he even ran into the middle of a street fight brandishing a crucifix aloft. As in the case of Fr Andrew, his spell of duty in Bethnal Green was an invaluable introduction to the rough-and-tumble of East End life, in which, like Andrew before him, he proposed to immerse himself once he had been ordained.

The remaining hurdle to surmount before ordination (since he had not read theology at Oxford) was a year at a theological college. On the advice of Winnington-Ingram he chose one with a Catholic background, Ely (again unconsciously following in Andrew's footsteps). He was there from May 1908 to June 1909. The East End had hardened him sufficiently to enable him to write to his mother soon after his arrival: 'I am not very much struck by the men, but I don't know them yet – I think *they* are alright, but the East End has changed *me*, so I shall have to get a little more acclimatised . . . Very little time to waste at Ely: it is regulated even down to ten minutes . . . I miss the East End horribly. This is a blooming monastery!'

Gordon's great friend Walter Carey, who had been at Ely eleven years before him, had come away with much the same impression: there were too many petty restrictions, and the teaching lacked vision. Some of the teachers, however, were better than others. Gordon was particularly influenced by the chaplain, Reginald (Rex) Palmer, a son of the then editor of the *Church Times* who was later to serve as a missionary in British Columbia and as a much-loved priest in the diocese of Oxford. Among Gordon's contemporaries at Ely were Thomas Crick, a future Dean of Rochester, and Walter Hughes, who was to spend most of his ministry as an army chaplain. Crick remembered Gordon as a 'quiet young man, not particularly expansive but with a happy sense of fun'. Hughes, who was one of an Evangelical minority at the college cold-shouldered as 'the Prots' by the Anglo-Catholic majority, was grateful to Gordon, 'whom we all knew as a very holy man', for his kindly refusal to join in the intolerance of his fellows.

On Trinity Sunday, 6 June 1909, he was ordained deacon by Bishop Jacob of St Albans for St Columba's, Wanstead Slip, in the Stratford Marshes – where, as Gordon's biographer observes, 'the slums of East London have begun to merge into middle-class or artisan respectability'. He was priested by Jacob on 22 May 1910 (and was able to give his sick father Communion on a number of occasions before the latter's death in October).

His vicar, Peter Barnes, to whom he had been recommended by his college principal, was a man of saintliness and humility to whom Gordon later acknowledged his deep debt. He soon began to realize that parish life was not really his metier. Nevertheless, for three years he was assiduous in carrying out his parochial duties – which included helping his fellow-curate and ex-Ely friend, Walter Hughes, with running the local Scout troop. '"Bull" [*Gordon's nickname at Ely had followed him to Stratford*] took a very great and friendly interest in the Scouts, and they would do anything for him; but running around in shorts was not his line. We all enjoyed his great sense of humour, and it was like a tonic to hear him laugh.' More to Gordon's taste were the mission services which he conducted outside public houses in the rougher parts of the district. According to Barnes he made more direct conversions during his short time in the parish than any other priest he had ever known – including at least one militant atheist whom Gordon converted to a living faith in Christ. Another of his converts declared: 'I would follow that man to the ends of the earth if I were told to do so.'* Gordon was also remembered in the parish long afterwards for the many hours he spent each week in private prayer and meditation in the church, often going there, whatever the weather, long before daybreak. He had no high opinion, however, of parish life as exercised in the Church of England at large. To his mother he wrote from Stratford: 'As I look at the life of the average English clergyman there seems to me to be no reason why our type should expect to convert the world, for we are not living the life in the kind of conditions suggested in the Gospels. Our life does not match the Bible account. Hence our failure'. This was stern criticism indeed. So it is hardly surprising that the high-principled Gordon Bulstrode should practise what he preached by distancing himself from the parish system and seek some more (to him) rewarding sphere of ministry. In the early summer of 1912 he determined to abandon St Columba's

---

* The man's wife, who was present, exclaimed: 'What! and leave me me!' 'Yes', he declared emphatically, 'even you!'

and try his vocation with the Society of St John the Evangelist – the Cowley Fathers. He left Stratford for Cowley on Michaelmas Day. His vicar wrote to Mrs Bulstrode: 'My sorrow at Gordon's departure is very great. The personal loss of his company is considerable . . . The loss to the parish is more serious, for he was God's instrument for the conversion of a great many . . . He is following what he is persuaded is the call of God'.

*   *   *

Gordon's decision to test his vocation had not been lightly reached. He had first come across the Cowley Fathers while at the university (the village of Cowley is only a few miles from Oxford) and had been immensely attracted by their way of life. At the same time an urge to detach himself spiritually from the world was bound up with a profound concern for the needs of the world's outcast and poor; and for some time he was torn by indecision as to whether to cast his lot with the Cowley Fathers or with the Franciscan-inspired Society of the Divine Compassion. The SDC house in Balaam Street, Plaistow, was within walking distance of Wanstead Slip; and during his curacy he made contact both with Fr William, the then Superior of the SDC, and with his successor, Fr Andrew. Gordon wrote later to a friend that 'dear Father Andrew greatly desired that I should go to Plaistow to try my vocation there, and was greatly disappointed that I went to Cowley instead'. For months Gordon dithered between the two communities. In January 1912 he wrote to his mother: 'I am still quite uncertain as to whether God wills Cowley or Plaistow; but I am sure He will show. His Love has never failed us for guidance yet'. In April he wrote again to her that, although he was sure by now that God was calling him to the form of renunciation required of a religious, 'the further advice I hope to take will not be on this point, but on the comparative detail as to which community to ask to accept me for a trial test and how soon it will be right to begin'.

In the end it may have been the influence of his vicar, Peter Barnes, which impelled Gordon into the arms of Cowley rather than Plaistow. For some reason Barnes had taken against the SDC and was therefore delighted when Gordon eventually decided to plump for the SSJE instead. 'I am so very glad that God seems to be guiding Gordon to go to Cowley rather than to the Society of the Divine Compassion', he wrote to Mrs Bulstrode on 12 July. 'I am prejudiced against the latter, and I have been finding it very hard to believe that it was for his good or the glory of God that he should join them.' Barnes added that, though Gordon might never be a bishop, he would have his intellectual side strengthened rather than weakened at Cowley. 'So he will become a more polished instrument for the carrying-out of God's work.' In the event all this agonizing between the rival attractions of the two communities proved academic, as (for reasons which will become apparent) Gordon soon found that he had misread God's promptings and that the monastic life as such was not for him. But, at the time, the choice must have seemed a genuine one.

His route from Stratford to Cowley was a roundabout one which took him first to Oswestry in Shropshire, where he had led a parish mission the previous year and where he now preached. From Oswestry he went on to stay with a cousin at Shrewsbury, and from there continued on foot. The trip took him five days (he stayed one night at a parsonage, another in a barn, and the remaining two in casual wards). Its significance lies in the fact that it taught him the joys and opportunities for an evangelist on the open road. He experienced great kindness and hospitality on this pioneer pilgrimage. In one village a 'dear Roman Catholic lad' ran after him and tried to press him to accept a sixpenny tip. Later he joined a semi-circle of the 'roughest men, women, children and babies you can imagine' round their camp-fire. Gordon improvised a short service for them. 'They *did* sing, and listened so beautifully, finishing with "Abide with me". I got stuck once or twice, but they prompted me and we went on gaily. At the end one of the very roughest men came up to me privately and tried to press some coins (2d., I think it was, all that he had) into my hand. I explained that I made it a rule not to beg (for this of course is punishable by law) or to accept money, but only to take food or hospitality as it was offered.'

No doubt the glimpses of real poverty Gordon encountered

on his hundred-mile journey hardened his almost obsessional horror of property and ownership. So, when he reached Cowley and learned that his father's will had been proved, he knew what he must do. Like all his brothers and sisters he received a legacy of £3000 – a sizeable sum of money in 1912. But he kept not a penny of this for himself, his only thought being how he could rid himself of such a financial burden. He appointed Peter Barnes as his 'almoner', directing him to divide the money between the neediest ex-employees at his late father's flour mills, ordination candidates and poor widows. He was intolerant of those who failed to share his own scorn of material possessions. Soon after the end of the First World War the family firm, now managed by two of his brothers, ran into financial difficulties and eventually into bankruptcy. Gordon was unsympathetic about his brothers' plight. 'Glory be to God!', he wrote sanctimoniously to his sister Alice. 'Now perhaps dear Frank will be able to give his whole mind to higher things!' His letter continued in the same vein:

> I ought to be praying that God may show us what is the meaning of all that is befalling our family. He has poured *great* benefits upon us; few in these days have had such blessings in parentage, home, upbringing; we have been spared the trials of poverty . . . Are there things in our relationship with each other, or in the business of life, which are displeasing Him? Have we prided ourselves as Bulstrodes, and thought ourselves better than others? . . . We must not be surprised, must we, if we are brought to real poverty? It is surprising how one dreads it; and yet it might be a very close union with our Blessed Lord.

Even Alice, a woman dedicated to hard work on behalf of others, was unable to go all the way with her brother in his total disregard for worldly possessions. After he had declared on one occasion that he had no home and that, if he were ill or became too old for work, he would expect to go to the workhouse infirmary, she retorted quite sharply: 'That is nonsense. Dear Brother knows quite well that my home is his home whenever he wants or needs it'. He did eventually swallow his pride and take up residence with her and their sister Emily at her home in

Slough; but that was only during his final illness, when, to his credit, he realized how much it would have hurt them if he had followed his inclination to end his days in a public infirmary for the old and dying. There is no doubt, however, that his dislike of all unnecessary expense was entirely genuine. On one occasion he even refused the gift of a cloak from a well-wisher because, he told his sister Alice, God had spoken to him in a dream and told him that he must not accept it. 'It had been a grief to me for a long time that I had two cloaks, one thick and one thin, so when they were wearing out I got one that would do equally well for summer or winter. Anything in the shape of a lighter cloak would be simply luxury.' This of course was in the days when real poverty was much more widespread than now and pitifully low wages were the norm. This was particularly so in the country. Gordon wrote to his mother in 1913: 'In the midst of cows the children get no milk and the people live very largely on bread and lard. No dripping, for they can't afford meat more than once a week . . . Most of the cottages seem "tied" to small farmers, who can give the people a week's notice and often do not allow them even to keep a pig lest they be robbed of pig-food'.

Gordon's arrival at Cowley in October 1912 marked a mile-stone in his life in more ways than one. Not only did it signify his complete renunciation of worldly possessions: it pointed the way to the next stage of his ministry as a roving evangelist. To begin with, however, there was no hint that he had arrived at a spiritual crossroads. He went through the normal three months as a postulant and then on 4 January 1913 was clothed as a novice with the Cowley habit. He enjoyed many of the aspects of the monastic life: the frequent services, the long periods of prayer and meditation, the retreats, even the housework and other domestic tasks. His mother and sister, visiting him from Oxford in the early summer, saw him seemingly happy and fulfilled and felt that he had really found his vocation. Appearances were deceptive, however. While Gordon – or rather Brother Edward, as he had now become – was perfectly happy to accept the two monastic vows of poverty and chastity, he baulked at the vow of obedience. He would, he said, usually be able to obey his Father-Superior, but this might not always be so: his prime obedience must always be to the guidance of God. In a crucial interview with the Superior, Gerald Maxwell, he asked if he could be excused from this vow. He was humble enough to admit that his own decisions would probably be less wise than those of the Superior., but he was clear that he could not risk taking a binding vow which he might feel compelled to break if a higher authority (i.e., God) so ordered. Not surprisingly Maxwell, faced with such an unorthodox request, turned it down and told the rash young novice that he would have to leave Cowley. Edward was undismayed. Later he came to believe that it was through God's guidance that he had not remained permanently with the Cowley Fathers. He was sure by now that God was calling him to a life in which he must be free to listen directly for the Divine guidance and not to depend for direction on fallible human beings. He must therefore undertake a free-lance ministry or maybe found a community of his own. In the end he did just that, even though his first attempt failed and the body which he subsequently helped to launch was not a religious community in the traditional sense.

The Village Evangelists, however, lay many years ahead. In July 1913 Edward found himself in effect thrown out of Cowley with no very clear idea of his next step. He had no wish to return to the parish ministry, and obviously could not approach another religious order requiring that awkward vow of obedience. Fired by his experience on the road from Shrewsbury, he hankered after the life of an itinerant preacher. He went at once to the Bishop of Oxford, Charles Gore, and put the idea before him, suggesting that he might be given some sort of a roving licence. Gore was unhelpful. He might, with his Anglo-Catholic sympathies, be prejudiced in favour of Brother Edward person-ally, but, as a bishop of the Church of England, he was too much wedded to the Establishment to take kindly to the idea of such an unconventional ministry as Edward proposed. The result of the interview was reported by Edward in a letter to his mother (24 July 1913): 'I saw the Bishop on Tuesday. His attitude was just what I had been told to expect: kind but damping. Not liking the idea, and not disposed in any way to take any responsibility either for the scheme or for me personally. He very much hoped that I should be able to realise my conditions of life either in one of the existing orders or as a curate. This leaves things very much where they were'. Edward was not too down-hearted, however, about this setback to his plans. He told his mother: 'I believe that it is that necessary splash of cold water through which anything which is unfamiliar but of God must struggle for its own testing and purification'. He accepted a few short-term posts (locums and suchlike) and moved from one place to another, though without seeming to have any clear idea of exactly where he was going. Then came a lucky break, brought about at the suggestion of his friend Walter Carey, by then a Librarian of Pusey House, Oxford.

Carey (1875–1955), who was one of eleven children, was a warmhearted, friendly and indisputably muscular Christian. He had been an Oxford rugger blue, had rowed for his college and loved gossiping to customers in a pub over a pint of beer. He also had a good brain and had narrowly missed gaining firsts at Oxford in both Mods and Greats. He was a friend of Gore and shared his social concern. He was later to win fame both as a naval chaplain at the Battle of Jutland and as Bishop of Bloemfontein in South Africa. He had known Edward since his Oxford days and was the priest to whom he had made that crucial first confession. Although he himself enjoyed the fleshpots of life and was very much a man of the world, he recognized the essential holiness of Brother Edward, his special quality of detachment from temporal issues and his concentration on the things of the spirit. He now came to the rescue of the ex-monk with a suggestion that was to have a profound effect on his future. The suggestion took the form of an introduction to a saintly but ailing priest, Frank Fairbairn, who, for nearly thirty years (1902–31), was Vicar of Temple Balsall, six miles from Coventry, Warwickshire, and Master of Temple Balsall Hospital. The 'hospital' was in fact a collection of almshouses built on a site at one time owned by the Knights Templar where thirty-six widows could be lodged on three sides of a quadrangle on the fourth side of which was the church. There were houses with gardens for a master and matron. The foundation dated from the seventeenth century and provided the inmates with a mixture of communal life and individual seclusion. Fairbairn and his wife Sophia were a remarkable couple who dedicated their lives to the building and cherishing of a Christian community life comparable to that of Little Gidding under Nicholas Ferrar. They held quiet days and retreats; and Frank was a generation ahead of his time in conducting a family communion service each Sunday followed by a parish breakfast. In some ways Sophia was the more unusual character of the two. A tiny woman (she used to say that she had been baptized in a sugar-basin), she was the daughter of an Indian general with the blood of the Bruce Kings of Scotland in his veins. Beneath her gentle and attractive exterior lay a hidden life of prayer and discipline rarely met with in modern times. She rose for prayer at 5.30 am in summer and winter alike. Each day, in addition to attending the Eucharist, Mattins and Evensong, she recited the entire Divine Office. For over thirty years she never touched food till teatime on Wednesdays and Fridays all the year round – though she showed great ingenuity in concealing this practice and would lay aside her austerities when visitors who would not understand them were in the house. Her intensely devotional and disciplined life was the mainspring of her ceaseless labours for others.

Walter Carey's acquaintance with the Fairbairns had arisen from the vicar's poor health. Fairbairn needed the services of a curate who could take charge when he was ill but who could occupy himself in other ways when Fairbairn was able to perform his duties himself. Carey had been assisting him for some months, but now needed to find a successor. Edward seemed to him ideally qualified to fill the role. It would provide him with a base, but leave him (assuming the vicar's health problems grew no worse) with sufficient leisure to conduct missions in different parts of the country as opportunity arose. The Fairbairns at once recognized Edward as a kindred spirit. Childless themselves, they called him 'Theodore' – the gift of God. Although Frank remained 'the dear vicar' to Edward throughout the time he was based at Temple Balsall, he always addressed Sophia as 'Little mother' and signed himself 'your son in Christ'. She was twenty

years older than him, but it may be that he intentionally stressed
the filial relationship as a protection against the risk of a more
emotional involvement. To both Edward and Sophia, brought
up as they had been according to the strict Victorian moral
code, any such romantic notions would have been anathema.
They remained firm and affectionate friends throughout their
lives; and the mother-son relationship was reflected both in
homely confidences on mundane matters and in frank discussions
on deeper issues.

Apart from an interlude of a few months in 1914–15 when he
was ministering to troops in Sussex, Edward made Temple
Balsall his base for fourteen years, and it became for him a
second home. The Fairbairns had private means, and their
general style of living was more comfortable (even allowing for
Sophia's austerities) than the ascetic Edward could really ap-
prove. But by now he was content to accept such people as they
were, and not to condemn them because they failed quite to
achieve his own ultra-high standards. As he put it in a letter
written to his mother shortly after his first arrival at Temple
Balsall: 'The outward circumstances of the life you see here have
more of almost luxury than I have shared in, to any extent,
before in my life. But the dear vicar and his wife have been
given grace to live the life of real detachment with real, thankful
appreciation of God's goodness and bounty, so I believe I shall
be given grace to learn it too in answer to your prayers'.
Edward certainly found the practicalities of the arrangement
ideal. In 1950, towards the end of his life, he wrote to his sister
Alice: 'For fourteen years I lived at Temple Balsall under the
Fairbairns' roof, sharing their wonderful prayer life, and I did all
I was allowed to do to help in the parish work when I was
there. But I never took on anything that required permanence –
a regular class, etc. – except perhaps for a month or so for a
special need. So that I was free to go out on retreats, missions,
etc., as invitations came'. Of the Fairbairns themselves he wrote
about the same time: 'They were saints, and there was a most
beautiful life of prayer and service going on in this Parish . . .
God sent me there to see country parish life in an almost ideal
form'. His longest absence from Temple Balsall was when he

was acting as an unofficial chaplain at an army camp in Sussex. Although lasting only five months, however, that chaplaincy proved a minefield for him.

*   *   *

When the First World War broke out in August 1914 Edward was about to join our old friend Brother Giles (the future founder of the Brotherhood of St Francis of Assisi) on a mission near Maidstone, Kent. The mission was to the slum-dwellers from East and South London who flocked down to the hopgardens of Kent in late summer. After the hop-season had ended the two men stayed on to help gather the harvest of Kentish cob-nuts. Their evangelistic efforts evidently proved fruitful. In a letter to Frank Fairbairn Edward was able to report enthusiastically:

> The daily Mass is changing the whole atmosphere in the huts; you never heard such an appalling drunken row and murderous quarrel as there was the first night in these huts. Now it is different, and last night by the open stick fire in the common cookhouse one of the parties to the quarrel was talking to me about the Mass and said, 'So you have Jesus Christ there to talk to you every morning', grasping the whole thing at once, D.G. They are all of that class which it is hard to reach except by some such way as this.

After the nut-picking had ended Giles urged Edward to consider re-entering a regular religious community. Edward wrote for advice to Fr Maxwell at Cowley, who suggested that he should come back there for a few weeks to think things out. More to the point, Maxwell offered to recommend him for an unofficial chaplaincy among the troops awaiting embarkation for France at Roffey Camp, near Horsham, Sussex. Edward warmed to the idea and went to Horsham in mid-December. He was given some sort of official standing by being appointed a temporary curate at the parish church. Unfortunately he soon found himself a fish out of water. He was full of enthusiasm, keen to be involved in the war effort and prepared to work himself almost to death. But his vicar was elderly, cautious, and suspicious of what he regarded as Edward's new-fangled notions such as a daily communion service. The officers were, with a few exceptions, polite but unenthusiastic. The men declined to flock in any great numbers to the special services and courses of instruction which Edward laid on for them. On the other hand they respected and liked him, and always gave him a welcome in their canteen and the YMCA recreation hut.

He never went out of his way to propitiate the authorities. On one occasion, when the colonel had cancelled a church parade because it was raining, Edward asked him whether the parade would have been cancelled if Lord Kitchener had been coming rather than God. But the colonel's chief objection to the unortho-dox young missioner arose from his pacifist views. In the ten years since he had left Keble Edward had become (like Fr Andrew) a convinced pacifist. At the same time he was (again like Andrew) honest enough to be able to see the other side of the coin. Years later he wrote of his wartime dilemma: 'It really was an agony. On the one hand, the more I meditated on Christ's life and example and on his teaching, the less did I find it possible to reconcile it with fighting and intentional slaughter. On the other hand, it was perfectly plain that some of the finest Christians – e.g., General Gordon and General Dobbie – were entirely without scruple in this matter, and that for the rank-and-file voluntary enlisting was the most unselfish and sacrificial thing they had ever done'. The vicar knew his views and asked him to avoid the subject of pacifism in his sermons to the troops. Edward replied that he cóuld not trammel the Holy Spirit if his guidance was otherwise. At least he had the satisfac-tion of not being an official chaplain and therefore subject to military discipline. As he wrote in a letter to his mother: 'I *do* find it so hard to keep the spiritual line with the dear Colonel and other people. I am sure that God has given me this position unfettered by any of the ordinary things which clog and bind most of us, e.g. being in the official employment and pay of people'. But independence in itself was not going to be enough to safeguard his position in the camp, and the end was not long delayed. Kenneth Packard, in his biography, puts it diplomatic-ally: 'Already the relations between Brother Edward and the military Command had become uncomfortable; a week or two later they had become acutely strained. A flare-up occurred; and Brother Edward did what was probably the only thing possible: he cut the Gordian knot and walked out'. Edward himself gives some more details in a letter to his mother dated 18 May 1915:

> I am now not allowed to speak any more to the troops in Horsham . . . The officers of the Artillery complained to the vicar that what I had said to the men the Sunday before last had had a depressing effect and they did not like what I had said about being men of peace. So the vicar asked me to take a certain line with them which I could not in faithfulness do. I *cannot* tell beforehand what the Lord shall put into my mouth. I try to ask the Holy Spirit to speak through me and I cannot limit His operation. So I offered to cease my ministrations and the offer was accepted. I am thankful to say there was no bitterness at all on either side, but simply the vicar took the service instead of me and my connection with the parish of Horsham has ceased.

Edward wasted no time in leaving the scene of his abortive labours. He tramped the thirty-five miles from Horsham to his mother's home at Southfields in a single day, arriving with his feet severely blistered. As he crossed the doorstep he fainted into his mother's arms. Ten days later he returned to Temple Balsall, which remained his home base until the late nineteen-twenties.

Once more his friends exerted themselves to try and 'place' him. His pacifist views, for some bishops, ruled him immediately out of court. Gore was more sympathetic when approached on Edward's behalf by Ernest Seyzinger, CR. 'The Bishop of Oxford was very kind and patient', Seyzinger wrote to Edward. 'He thinks, and I agree with him, that you should make a centre in some *one* parish to begin with; and go out from that to spend bits of time in other parishes for preaching or itinerary work, or any other ministry that may offer'. In effect Edward was to do exactly that for the foreseeable future, choosing Temple Balsall as his parish centre. He divided his time between deputizing for the vicar during the latter's bouts of ill-health and conducting missions and retreats outside the parish. But, before considering these external activities, which were to lead many years later to the launching of the Village Evangelists, one must jump ahead a bit in time: to Edward's ill-starred attempt to found a community of his own when Westcote replaced Temple Balsall as his parochial base.

For some time he had been hoping to establish a centre where both men and women could be trained as 'friar-evangelists' and go out, either singly or in pairs, to take the gospel to the country parishes of England. As early as 1917 he had mentioned in a letter to his mother how wonderful it would be to have a form of corporate living without vows. The thought of the vow of obedience continued to frighten him off any attempt to resume the traditional religious life. When, in 1923, Geraldine Mott, one of a group of sympathizers to whom he had given the collective name of the Servants and Handmaids of Jesus of Nazareth, mentioned to him her attraction towards the 'religious ideal', he told his sister Alice that he was not led that way.

> I shall tell her that her course is to ask some community to train her for beginning a community on the lines she indicates. I cannot have any responsibility for it myself. It was this issue, I think, that was at the back of my coming away from Cowley, and it was this quite distinctly which made it impossible for me to go on with Brother Giles. He could only contemplate life as a 'religious', and I felt sure God had brought me from it as out of Egypt. My contention – it may be my pride – is that the third vow, of obedience, may be needed as a mortification of self-will, but is not a counsel of perfectionism on all fours with the call to celibacy and poverty which we have our Lord's own words for. It is when it is exalted to this level that I run up against it.

It was Edward's inability to jump the fence of obedience that prevented him joining even the Brotherhood of St Francis of Assisi, which, in the nineteen-twenties and thirties, was getting into its stride at Hilfield, Dorset, under Douglas Downes, and with whose ideals Edward so profoundly sympathized. Its aims and methods were exactly like his own, and its members, like him, spent much time tramping the roads and ministering to the outcasts of society. Edward often stayed with them, sharing in their missions and retreats as they shared in his, but could never bring himself to join even a community as close to his heart as this. He still found himself unable to give his total allegiance to a group of fallible human beings; he felt that it would both stifle his freedom and offer him a security which he had no desire to accept. The only source of dependence on which he wished to rely was God.

But community living without the strings of obedience attached was a very different matter. And so, when an opportunity arose in 1927, he seized it eagerly. The human intermediary on this occasion was the Revd John Arthur Thomas, who had been Rector of Westcote, a village in the Cotswolds, since 1906. He had invited Edward to lead a mission to his parish, and after the mission told him of a large cottage for sale in the village that had been built as a 'roadhouse' but had failed because it was too far from a main road. To the rector it seemed to have possibilities as a centre for prayer and retreats. To Edward it seemed a heaven-sent opportunity of realizing his dream of a training-place for his evangelists; but the problem was where to find the necessary funds with which to buy it. It was here that Geraldine Mott came to the rescue. She had sufficient capital to purchase both the former roadhouse and a smaller cottage behind the church. The first was renamed Bethlehem and the other Nazareth. The latter became the nucleus of a men's community under Edward himself and Bethlehem a women's community under Miss Mott, now styled Mother Geraldine. The life of both houses was to centre on the parish church, where the men and the women were to say all the offices together, as at Temple Balsall. At the same time both cottages were to keep an ever-open door, so that 'the sick, the sinful, and the sad might come to be helped'. There was no guaranteed income. 'We live from day to day and leave the rest to God', said Edward. Such was the theory. How did it all work out in practice?

Kenneth Packard calls the story of Westcote 'an heroic failure', and so it was in the sense that the twin communities never developed in the way envisaged by Edward. But, though the men's side came to grief after only a few years, the women at Bethlehem survived much longer. The root cause for Westcote's failure to develop in the way intended was due partly to the natural dangers inherent in a mixed community, partly to a fundamental difference of opinion between Edward and Geraldine over the definition of a religious community, and partly to Edward's frequent absences from Westcote. It appears that the women soon felt the need for the more orthodox support of vows taken and of discipline imposed from without as well as from within. Geraldine thought that, in a religious community, certain rules of the house were necessary, such as set times for meals, for getting up and for going to bed, and a proper timetable of duties to be performed. Edward, though always willing to fit in with domestic arrangements and join in the liturgy, found it irksome to be trammelled by even a limited amount of additional routine.

He made his position clear in a series of letters to Sophia Fairbairn. On 20 September 1930 he writes to express his dismay that she was finding it difficult to distinguish Westcote from a traditional religious community. 'Father Thomas holds that our consecration is a vow, though terminable at any time. If it is so, it is entirely different from what I meant and to what I have steadily declared to all comers and to our supporters, and do still. If we are people under vows, I have said I see no alternative to retiring from the Society.' Edward told Sophia that, in his view, a vow must have a time-limit, and that a person under a vow for, say, a year must exclude all thoughts foreign to the vow till the expiration of that year. 'This is not so with us. It has its difficulties, I confess, but it has great safeguards. We are free to reconsider at any time . . . It is this that is behind my real anguish about the clothes. I feel it is not honest to try to get a uniform as near as possible like a "religious". In a way we are like permanent novices of a religious society, living by the rules but not bound by the vows.'

Edward contended that the life of an evangelist was a thing distinct, though it had much to learn from the religious. It depended not on vows, but on non-binding counsels. 'Our training would not satisfy any religious community as a novitiate. A community we are. That is a general term. By our common rule, life and purse we are truly a community . . . If people call us an evangelist community they are giving a true description. "Religious" in the ordinary, wide sense I hope we may be – at all events not irreligious; but "religious" in the technical sense we are not, and I hope we may never be.'

Differences of opinion over what constituted a religious community were not the only ones to surface at Westcote. There were human problems as well. The men and women slept in different houses, but worked and prayed together throughout the day; and attachments were inevitably formed which directed attention away from the total dedication envisaged by Edward and which sometimes led to a conflict of loyalties. While Edward was on the spot, his holiness, gentleness and loving-kindness helped to surmount the difficulties. But he was so often away on retreats, missions or preaching engagements that any troubles which surfaced during his absence tended not to go away. Such problems might include personality clashes, love affairs, doubts over decision-making, and even resentment of whatever authority figure might be installed at Westcote to deputize for Edward. For a time he relied on the services of his sister Alice and brother Frank, who let their house in Slough and moved to Westcote to help with the new venture. Their rush to assist their brother may have been due more to the enthusiasm of Alice than to that of Frank, who left the community fairly soon. Alice stuck it out rather longer, ministering to the needs of the men at Nazareth. She, like Edward, was a gentle, loving person, but she needed cherishing and was easily hurt. As her role at Westcote was to cherish rather than be cherished, eventually she found the strain too great and left.

For a time Edward had hopes of Brother Donald (Rendall), whom he left in charge during his frequent absences. He wrote a whole series of letters to Donald filled with maxims of guidance and support. But Donald was only in his early twenties and not mature enough to live up to the precepts of his mentor. He frequently found himself the only occupant of Nazareth, could not get on with Alice Bulstrode, and was often lonely and depressed. He failed to profit from Edward's perpetual letters of advice and, after little more than two years, packed it in. He left in September 1930. Edward reproached himself for his inability to keep Donald at Westcote. 'I feel D. is the only real spiritual son God has given me', he wrote to Sophia. 'There will not be another. The Lord gave and the Lord hath taken away. Blessed be the name of the Lord.'* There were never more than two or three men at a time at Nazareth. By 1932 they had all drifted away. The house was left empty until it was taken over by the Cowley Fathers and renamed St John's Cottage.

The story of Bethlehem was a happier one in the sense that it kept going after the collapse of Nazareth, albeit in the form of an orthodox convent whose members took vows and wore a religious habit. Mother Geraldine had no difficulty in attracting recruits, and during its forty-two-year history (1927–69) twenty-four Sisters were professed in her Community of Jesus of Nazareth. The community was unusual in that, like its male counterpart, it lived on faith alone. Its members brought nothing with them and were allowed no income. They relied on prayer, hard work and donations to sustain both them and their missions.

On one occasion a large and needy family moved into the village. When she heard the news Geraldine ordered that the community's lunch – roast joint and plum pie – be sent round to them immediately. The Sisters were dismayed, but offered up fervent prayers. The next morning, on the refectory steps, they found two rabbits and a bag of plums! Life at Bethlehem was spartan. Initially there was no heating whatever in the building except on Christmas Day, and every winter the pipes froze and burst. Regular fires were not introduced until the 1940s, and water at first had to be pumped by hand in the yard and carried indoors.

The Sisters' chief activity was helping priests in their parishes. 'We were like sheepdogs, going out and rounding up interest in parishes', a Sister once quipped. They confined themselves to spiritual matters, however. It was not part of their vocation or

---

*Donald, of Scottish parentage, was a former Church Army cadet who had first met Edward during a mission at Leek, Staffordshire. After leaving Westcote he served for five years as a lay brother at Cowley. Edward always retained a great affection for him and kept up a correspondence with him for the rest of his life.

duty to undertake social work – though if, in the course of their mission work, they discovered cases of mental distress and material privation, they referred them to the appropriate charity or agency. When not engaged in external duties they toiled away at their household tasks – cooking, washing, cleaning and growing their own vegetables. By the end of the 1930s their work was becoming widely known in the Church at large, and their services were much in demand.

In 1955 Mother Geraldine suffered a near-fatal heart-attack and had to resign as Superior.* Her place was taken by Mother Mary Theodore from West Malling in Kent. During the 1960s the community declined in numbers and influence, and found it increasingly difficult to maintain its work. In 1969 the surviving members joined the Sisters of Charity at Knowle, near Bristol. The convent, which had been much enlarged over the years, was sold to a property company in 1971 and converted into seven houses. But the community's memory lives on in the patronal names which various houses and fields in Westcote still bear – Nazareth Field, St Agnes, St Julien and so on. During their forty years' residence the Sisters brought a continuous stream of visitors to Westcote and are still remembered by the older villagers with respect and affection.

*   *   *

Brother Edward first took part in parish missions while he was still at Oxford, and it was in this type of work that he found his true vocation. He was ready to accept any invitation, to answer any call, and to preach the Word of God in any place. He was entirely dependent for his food and lodging on private hospitality. His conception of a mission to a parish was that it should be something more like a 'blitz' than an effort demanding long and

---

*The esteem in which Mother Geraldine was held was such that, when news of her heart-attack reached the commander of the nearby aerodrome, he ordered his planes to be temporarily grounded in order to give her some peace. One runway, which led directly over the convent, was closed at night for some weeks until she was out of danger. She continued to live at the convent till 1960, when, accompanied by two fellow-Sisters, she moved into a bungalow at Crossways, Dorset. She died in 1976.

detailed preparation – which, he thought, could possibly stultify or quench the fire of the Spirit. He loved to chat with folk at bus-stops and (if the landlord agreed) in pubs. One bus passenger was surprised, when he joined a long queue at a bus-stop in pouring rain, to find everyone laughing and singing a hymn – under the direction of a black-robed priest in a black hat with a wide, curly brim. It was the irrepressible Brother Edward. On a June night, when he was addressing a crowd in London's Trafalgar Square, they were moved on by the police. 'We will go', Edward agreed, 'but first we will say a prayer for all policemen.'

Of course the conditions under which Edward conducted his missions were easier than they would be now. The majority of married women were at home during the day and, with few labour-saving devices, spent a great deal of their time on household chores. In the days before television their knowledge of the outside world might be limited. In this environment a mission in a country parish was an event of great local interest even to non-churchgoers, and an unexpected visitor during the day a welcome interruption to loneliness and drudgery. Conditions today are much less propitious to successful evangelism. The unexpected visitor is often an unpopular interruption either to a favourite TV or radio programme or to the chance to catch up on household jobs by the many who have been out at work all day. It was partly the changing social climate which led to a waning interest in parochial missions and to the eventual collapse of the Village Evangelists in the 1960's. But, while Edward was in his prime, evangelistic missions were very much a part of the parochial scene and Edward therefore found himself in his element.

During the period between the wars he spent a fair amount of his time in London, and in particular at the church of St Silas, Pentonville, near the Angel, Islington – 'between "The Angel" and "The Cross"' [i.e., King's Cross], as he used to describe its position to friends wishing to track him down. His association with the parish, one of the poorest in London and a hotbed of crime, dated from 1923, when he conducted a mission in Islington; and he used it as an occasional base for his work during the

1930s after the Fairbairns had left Temple Balsall. He was lent a little 'cell' over the church room where he could compile his Bible notes, deal with his correspondence and meet his friends. For his sustenance they would put little gifts of food in a box outside the door. For food, as for lodging, he continued to rely on God working through charitable individuals. If none was offered he went without, offering his hunger to God.* When in London he slept sometimes on the Embankment, sometimes in the crypt of St Martin's-in-the-Fields, sometimes in a casual ward. He found both casual wards and trains ideal openings for evangelism. His sermons generally took the form of telling a story, followed by some comments on the story. He was diffident in his preaching, never imposed himself on his hearers, and spoke with words which might be few but were very much to the point.

Another important part of Edward's peripatetic ministry was the conducting of retreats. He soon became a past-master at this particular form of spiritual exercise. Joanna Kelley found that one great difference between retreats led by Edward and those led by other conductors lay in the amount of time he allowed for silent prayer and meditation. 'In other retreats there are often three or four addresses each day plus prayers, many of which are said aloud by the conductor. One of the reasons that I remember so much of what Brother Edward said during retreats was because one had plenty of time to turn over in one's mind what one had heard and to let it sink into one's whole being.' Joanna Kelley found Edward a spellbinding story-teller. 'He did not need any of the techniques of introducing lighter touches or interspersing a talk with any sort of variety of programme. He sat in an upright chair with his small and well-worn Bible in his hands, his eyes looking lovingly at the retreatants. He always displayed a certain diffidence to start with, fearing lest he might

---

*When the Westcote experiment came to an end and Edward resumed his life as a wandering friar his meals became even more irregular and often indigestible. Years of being out in all weathers and often sleeping rough also took their toll on his health. In 1935 he collapsed with a perforated duodenal ulcer and was rushed to Chelmsford Hospital for an immediate operation. He made a good recovery, but his health thereafter often gave rise to anxiety.

be in some way interrupting a meditation or making it more difficult for the Holy Spirit to speak directly to a heart.' As his thought unfolded, however, he carried his hearers along, so that they felt they were living in the story and knew the characters. 'I remember once after a retreat talking about Moses to a colleague, who said: "You sound as if you had known him". I replied without thinking: "Oh no, *I* didn't know him, but he was a great friend of a friend of mine"!'

How did Edward strike the onlooker who met him for the first time? When Donald Rendall knew him he was clean-shaven and had a long, Italian-shaped face. His hair was beginning to thin. His eyes, a warm brown, were his best feature: expressive, clear and luminous. As Donald put it, 'his soul looked out at you'. Others who came across Edward made the same point. The first thing that struck Allan Dewar, a medical doctor and lay reader, was that 'loving expression of his eyes and his remarkable likeness to the traditional figure of our Lord'. Later Dewar visited Edward in London and was much struck by the sight of his friend from afar:

> There he was in the distance: a tall, stately figure in a cassock and hatless, with his lovely beard and the same wonderful expression on his features, standing by my open tourer Morris car in the midst of a countless throng of costers and their barrows, women and children in their gaily coloured scarves and ribbons, dogs and a few horses and carts, and a babel of voices shouting their wares to sell. There he stood, dignified and looking from side to side to see if he could get a glimpse of me. I could have believed it was Jesus Himself. Certainly Jesus was not very far away.

It will be noted that, by this time, Edward was sporting a beard. It dated, apparently, from the latter part of his Westcote period. Both the Rector of Westcote (J.A. Thomas) and the Vicar of St Silas's, Pentonville (E.T. Baker), claimed the distinction of having persuaded him to grow a beard: the former on the ground that it was more in keeping with the work of a missioner, the latter on the assumption that a young priest (as he still was then) would be less attractive to the young ladies if bearded! According to Joanna Kelley, however, there was a more mundane reason: 'He used to say that he had allowed his beard to grow because he did not then have to carry a razor'. Certainly, by the time she knew him towards the end of his life, a beard was very much a feature of his facial landscape. Here is her description of him after their first meeting:

> He was tall and slender, his forehead high, and he had large grey eyes which looked out lovingly at everyone. His hair and rather luxuriant beard were black. His elegant hands with long slender fingers reminded me of those Byzantine figures on the west porch of Chartres Cathedral.* His fine and clear voice had a considerable range, though he spoke quietly. I knew with instinctive certainty that the beauty of his appearance was the natural outcome and a manifestation of his holiness.

But, if Edward was a saint, he was a saint with his feet on the ground. He always wore a cassock because it was the cheapest form of clothing he could find. It also meant that he could wash out his shirts without having to iron them, since they did not show – an important saving of time in the days before the invention of drip-dry clothing.

Part of Edward's appeal lay in his unpartisan attitude to religious controversy. He wandered from camp to ecclesiastical camp, equally at home in all and recognizing that all, in their different ways, were seeking God. Once, when asked whether he belonged to the High Church or Low Church party, he replied: 'I have forgotten'. In his later ministry he combined an Evangelical, almost a Revivalist, appeal with very definite Catholic principles (here he resembled the celebrated Fr Ignatius). If asked what he thought about some particular point of doctrine he would give an honest reply and add: 'It is as God has shown me. Of course he may have guided you along different lines'. At a time when ecclesiastical opponents occupied deeply entrenched positions (as they still do!), his uncensorious diffidence provided a refreshing contrast. He was interested neither in church politics

---

*Towards the end of his life he suffered from rheumatoid arthritis, and his hands, with their elegant fingers, became misshapen, knobbly and increasingly useless. Holding a pen was then a difficult and painful task.

nor in church government. He always felt uncomfortable, however, about the Church of England's rich endowments and the immense cost of maintaining the fabric of its numerous parish churches. He argued that God would provide what was necessary, if asked, and that the Church's endless preoccupation with money set a very bad example to the nation as a whole.

He thought the case for the Church's disestablishment a strong one, for, in his view, a Church that was identified with the State could not always remain true to its first loyalty – God. He often found himself in obstinate opposition to the Establishment, but insisted that rigid conformity impeded the work of the Holy Spirit. Throughout his ministry he aimed to be a pilgrim without material ties. To live and worship as closely as possible after the pattern of our Lord was all that really mattered: the method by which this was achieved was of secondary importance. Edward's views on the priesthood were ahead of his time. He was all in favour of ordination, but considered that many priests might witness more effectively through working in secular employment. He was also ahead of his time in believing that vows taken by members of the established religious orders should be for limited periods of time only; they should be renewable, but not necessarily for life. Sometimes, he claimed, the spirit had gone out of a monk or a nun, and only constraint was left. He seldom read anything but the Bible, especially in his later years. He once wrote: 'People tend to read too much about religion and do not read God's word enough, just as it is more important to pray than to read books about prayer.*

Edward was a great believer in the ministry of healing, which in his early days had largely lapsed in the Church of England. He was happy to practise what he preached. Stephen Parsons, in his book *The Challenge of Christian Healing* (1986), records a personal experience of healing at Edward's hands which had

---

*Over a period of years Brother Edward wrote a series of Bible notes which were sent to anyone who wished to receive them. A.F. Edwards, later Secretary of the Coventry Council of Churches, testified to their value to him as a young man: 'Their uncompromising directness precisely matched my need. Here was a mode of interpretation of the Scriptures which I had never before taken seriously . . . here was allegory so rooted in the Incarnation that it led to the most practical action'.

happened to him before he was able to be conscious of it. 'My mother tells me that as a small child of eighteen months I was once plagued by a chronic attack of mastoiditis for which the doctor was recommending an operation. Brother Edward of the Village Evangelists was staying with us at our vicarage in Portsmouth, and he prayed with me. The pain went almost instantly, as assessed by the speed with which I fell asleep, and the operation was never performed.'

On one doctrinal issue Edward made no concessions to popular taste. This was the personal return of Christ to the world. He believed implicitly in the Second Coming and, during the last twenty years of his life, felt an increasing urge to preach about it. He soon became known as the prophet of the Second Coming, and was twitted by his friends for regarding it as 'the bee in his holy bonnet'. He cared nothing about such kindly criticisms, but rather gloried in them. No mission or retreat was complete without a long sermon on the subject, so deeply did he feel the urgency of his message.

In a preface to *Behold Thy King Cometh*, a symposium of essays on the Second Coming which he edited and which was published in 1950, he traces the strength of his conviction to the influence of two of the Cowley Fathers who shared it: R.M. Benson and F.W. Puller. Another doctrine which he preached as a corollary to this belief was that the purpose of the Church was not to 'convert' the world but simply to bear witness in every part of the world. He believed the vast majority of Christian believers to be in error on this question. There was no Scriptural warrant, in his view, for concluding that the Church's proclamation of the gospel would meet with universal acceptance. It was God who, in his mercy, would do the converting in his own time and way. Edward had long ago given up the idea that the world was going to get better and better and that, when all had been converted, Christ would come in his glory to be welcomed by a world consisting almost entirely of adoring believers. The true purpose of Christian witness, as Edward saw it, was to call out from each place and nation a people prepared for the Lord. Only when this 'number of the elect' had been made up would Christ be able to enter on the next main stage of his redemptive task – that of gathering the nations under his rule in the age to come.

In a message addressed to his fellow Village Evangelists three months before his death Edward referred to his well-known belief in our Lord's personal return to judge the world and continued: 'Many people think I am a crank in this matter; but I would ask them to remember that, when your self-starter will not work, you may be very thankful for a "*crank*"! And I reflect that St John the Baptist must often have wondered whether he was not misinterpreting prophecy and letting pride delude him into thinking that he was "The Voice". Yet God held him to his vocation, and we are thankful that he did not return to exercise his hereditary priesthood in Jerusalem and to exchange (as we might say) his raiment of camel's hair for a DD hood or the wilderness for a cathedral stall'. John's work, Edward concluded, had been to call out a people prepared for the Lord; and this, he believed, was the work of the Church in general and of Village Evangelism in particular. 'I believe that God has raised up VE at *this particular time* (he was writing in late 1952) to "prepare the way of the Lord by preaching and repentance".'

*　　*　　*

The Village Evangelism movement, which had been launched four years earlier, seemed a natural extension of Edward's own ministry. Its origins lay in his long-standing friendship with Walter Carey – the priest to whom he had made his first confession all those years ago. Carey had resigned as Bishop of Bloemfontein in 1934 because of ill-health and had taken up a post back in England as Chaplain of Eastbourne College. In 1947 Edward wrote to him to say that he felt led by the Holy Spirit to abandon his own single-handed role as a twentieth-century John the Baptist and instead to launch out on a wider evangelistic scale. He asked the bishop to go with him to a three-day retreat at Warlingham in Surrey to see if they could discover God's will in the matter. Seven others joined them at the retreat – including a certain Miss Evelyn Gedge. The conference got off to a bad start. For its first forty-eight hours it seemed, according to Edward, 'to be all at sixes and sevens'. There was disagreement and even bitterness. Then, after a night of continuous prayer, 'the most wonderful thing happened: God brought out of our muddles and bickering a new unity and a new hope'. The conference was of one mind as to what ought to be done. As Carey said afterwards: 'We were meant to stop passing resolutions deploring juvenile delinquency, or the apathy of the public towards religion, or the faults of anybody else, and instead *to do something ourselves*'.

Early in 1948 a further meeting was held at St Leonard's-on-Sea, Sussex. It was decided to form a small society of priests, to be called the Servants of Jesus of Nazareth, who would, together with a few layfolk, be prepared to go out into the countryside each year and conduct ten-day missions in groups of villages. Edward envisaged the idea as a form of 'spiritual first-aid'. To Carey (as he expressed it in his unsophisticated, no-nonsense manner) the object of the visitations was to tell the villagers that 'something was wrong with England and something was wrong with the souls of men – and that the only remedy was to get God back into England and into souls, and souls and England back into God'. At a further conference at Farnham Castle it was decided to drop the original title of Servants of Jesus of Nazareth and rechristen the venture 'the Village Evangelists' or 'Village Evangelism'.

In the movement's early years the VEs – as they soon became known – enjoyed an extraordinary success. Their numbers rose rapidly. By 1951 there were 350 of them – 250 priests and 100 lay men and women. At the peak of the movement, in the late 1950s, as many as a thousand people were involved in this voluntary, part-time evangelistic effort. Between 1948 and 1964 no fewer than four thousand parishes – roughly a third of the Church of England's total tally – received a visit from the Village Evangelists. They always waited to be asked. Parishes were never expected to have a mission thrust upon them against their inclinations. Each year about 250 missions were held.

Although the VEs as a group transcended ecclesiastical divisions, prospective helpers were often told whether a parish to be visited supported the Society for the Propagation of the Gospel (High Church) or the Church Missionary Society (Low Church). This was to enable them to choose, if necessary, parishes with whose views they were likely to find themselves in sympathy.

Sometimes the Holy Spirit directed otherwise. On one occasion Joanna Kelley remembers an elderly and saintly Evangelical cleric who had volunteered to assist in a mission to an Anglo-Catholic parish, and who came to Brother Edward before the final Eucharist of the mission with tears streaming down his face. 'He said he was prepared to wear a vestment and turn his face to the East for the Creed, which he had never done previously, because he had realised suddenly how little the outward trappings mattered where the Holy Spirit dwelt.'

Village Evangelism seemed to appeal mainly to people who had been brought up in the Christian tradition, of whatever persuasion. The usual result of a mission was an increase in the depth of church – and chapel – life. Many returned to the fold who had lapsed from regular prayer and worship, while existing churchgoers found their faith both strengthened and enriched. Parish magazines of the period carried articles describing the invigorating effect of a VE mission on the worshipping life of the parish. One comment common to almost all the articles was the wonderful spirit of fellowship engendered by the mission among the missioners themselves. 'In this fellowship', a missioner wrote, 'we were able to do things we thought we could never do, because we were doing them in the power and wisdom of the Holy Spirit.' In that particular village of fifteen hundred souls there were nearly two hundred worshippers at the early Communion service on the final Sunday of the mission; and a much larger number who followed the missioners through the village in a procession of witness after the closing service in the evening. The missioners usually wore bright red flannel crosses, about three inches long, on their coats, so that everyone could recognize them. They would arrive several days before a mission began, in order to reassure the doubters on the PCC and generally familiarize themselves with the parochial scene.

Many of the missioners might, at the start of a mission, be almost as timid as some of those they were to address. Edward recognized that this might be so and did his best to strengthen the faint-hearted with words of encouragement. 'We must speak from the heart and to the heart', he exhorted, 'and not be afraid of too much emotionalism. Especially the emotion-shy English must try to speak out, to show we really do love our Lord above all else. This love has driven us out to seek others and to love them. It is fervour that kindles and fire is needed'. Edward used to warn people after a mission to expect the Devil to run a sort of counter-mission. 'If you recognize it for what it is, you can take appropriate action and not let it worry you. Satan is very anxious to divert good work and to undo any good impression made.'

Of course Village Evangelism didn't just spring into life fully formed. It required patting into shape; and it was here that Walter Carey really came into his own. He was a born organizer; and, under his enthusiastic leadership, VE became a fully-fledged movement with its energies properly directed at the target. Carey wrote articles about VE in the Church newspapers which brought in both a flood of volunteers and countless pleas from parishes. The movement was obviously responding to a deeply-felt need. Edward himself, however, was always a little doubtful about the wisdom of these developments. He was terrified of over-organization, and once remarked: 'As soon as a movement has a treasurer and headed notepaper it loses its vitality and becomes stuck, like Lot's wife, who clung to the past'. He got his way inasmuch as the movement never did have a treasurer: enough money always seemed to come in to cover expenses, and any surplus was given away. It also managed to the end to do without headed notepaper, though the name and address of Evelyn Gedge, the honorary secretary (or 'correspondent', as she preferred to be called), was printed on gummed paper and stuck by her on whatever piece of paper she was using. Miss Gedge was indefatigable and managed the whole of the administration single-handed. She was the only whole-time (though always voluntary) member of staff. She contrived to please both her masters simultaneously: Bishop Carey by her organizing ability and Brother Edward by her prayerfulness, which reassured him that the Holy Spirit remained in absolute control.

She was a remarkable woman in her own right. She was the daughter of a former Vicar of Rochester, Kent; but her father had literally never seen her, as he had gone blind while on his honeymoon. As a girl she had been his constant and devoted

guide and companion, reading aloud to him, leading him through
the streets on his parish visits and supporting him in his every
endeavour. She was educated at St Paul's School for Girls and
afterwards at Girton College, Cambridge, where she took a first
in classics. She soon found that she needed only three or four
hours' sleep a night, so was able to pursue two careers simultaneously: as a full-time parish worker and as Secretary of Westfield
College, London. She also enjoyed an intense devotional life,
spending four hours each night (from about 3am to 7am) in
prayer, meditation and study of the New Testament (always in
Greek). She retired from Westfield in 1948, just at the time
when the VE movement was being launched, and joined it with
whole-hearted enthusiasm. Joanna Kelley, who knew her well,
recalls that it was her energy, drive and organizing ability that
enabled the movement to meet all the calls that were made upon
it. In the course of VE's life she must have driven many scores
of thousands of miles in her small grey Ford car, renewed each
year, which served as an office and in which, on a portable
typewriter, she dealt with her correspondence. When necessary
the car became her home in which she ate and slept. She seemed
to Mrs Kelley to have the look of a Raphael Madonna – a pure
and beautiful classical profile, sparkling brown eyes and a merry
expression. She usually wore a shabby blue cotton dress, a dark
blue cardigan and a blue veil.

In her ceaseless task of relating offers of service to requests
for missions Evelyn Gedge had her own inimitable epistolary
style and her own unfathomable system of using different-col-
oured bits of paper ('I enclose a pink'). She had a rapid mind,
and her ideas were so prolific that she moved from one to
another with such speed that it was sometimes impossible to
take in more than a fraction of what she said. Mrs Kelley draws
an amusing picture of Gedge in action:

> She seemed to talk in a sort of shorthand. She seldom used the
> pronoun 'I', but usually referred to herself as 'this handmaid' or
> 'this unworthy servant' or 'slave Gedge'; but she sparkled with so
> much merriment that one never knew if this convention was a
> joke or not. Her conversation was rather like a machine-gun,

emitting long, rapid, staccato bursts of fire in which some of the bullets found their mark every time. After a session with her I used to find that I needed several hours of sound sleep, so exhausted was I by the vain effort of trying to keep up with her.

She was variously known in VE circles as the Battle-Axe, the Bull-Dozer and the Dam-Buster. But, after Brother Edward's death, she may be said to have been the inspiration which kept the movement going – even though, in her own eyes, VE was the orchestra and she herself but a humble instrument.

* * *

Edward survived the formation of the VEs by only four years; but it was long enough for him to see the movement get fully into its stride. By this time he was known the length and breadth of the country and was still in constant demand as a missioner. He also achieved fame as a radio broadcaster. Such was his reputation that he was chosen to broadcast the opening address of the great Mission to London in 1949 from St Marylebone Parish Church. He was the only preacher acceptable to churchpeople of all schools of thought – and was allowed the rare privilege by the BBC of preaching an unscripted sermon. Every evening during the week of the mission over two thousand people crowded into St Marylebone church to hear his addresses. But by this time his health was in sharp decline. In January 1952 he collapsed during a retreat and spent three months at St Luke's Hospital in London. After a short spell in the country he went back to his sister Alice's house at Slough, where he remained until shortly before his death. The end came very suddenly on 25 March – Lady Day – 1953. He was being driven by ambulance to Windsor Hospital to be treated for his rheumatoid arthritis, but was taken seriously ill on the way. He was admitted to the hospital and died about 11 o'clock that night, the cause of death being a sudden haemorrhage of his gastric ulcer. Shortly before he died he regained consciousness for a short spell and whispered to his sister Alice: 'I don't want to get better; I want to go to Jesus'. His wish was speedily granted. He was aged 67.

At the beginning of her unpublished memoir Joanna Kelley remarks: 'In the course of my life I have known many good and saintly people, but only this one completely holy man'. Although she later discovered, as she sorted through his letters, that he was a much more complex and enigmatic character than she had realized, she found no reason to revise her verdict. Brother Edward might at times display a dedication to his task that amounted to fanaticism, but he contrived to keep his sense of balance. He seemed in perfect equilibrium, free, happy and fulfilled. He became, says Mrs Kelley, imbued with holy joy. 'One does not have to be holy, or even to wish to be holy, oneself to recognize it in another. Many besides myself who were moved by meeting Brother Edward and recognized this quality in him admitted that it denoted a way of life to which they had no real wish to aspire. It was impossible to meet him without being aware of the beauty of his life.' Bishop Carey made the same point in a different way in his autobiography (published two years before Edward's death) when he remarked: 'Brother Edward is practically unknown to important people. Members of Parliament don't lisp his name, nor do trades unionists reckon him at all. Yet he is one of the most influential people in England along his own lines as a John the Baptist, an inspirer of thousands, a saver of a multitude of souls. He was the son of rich parents, but abandoned everything for the life of a wandering preacher and has been such for nearly thirty years. He is simply the most Christ-like man I know'.

Evelyn Gedge once said that she detected in Edward a certain remoteness on the human level – he was not what nowadays would be called 'cosy'. But, to the anonymous reviewer of Kenneth Packard's 'life' in the *Ripon Diocesan Magazine*, he was 'completely approachable; he had time for everyone'. Nevertheless, said the reviewer,

> If you ever had the good fortune to meet Brother Edward, or even for that matter to see him, you will certainly retain in your memory as long as you live a recollection of the startling impression, akin to shock, which his appearance made on you. It wasn't his old patched blue habit, or his ample beard, both of which

were pleasantly unusual, but a presence – as though one stood before the burning bush. His appearance was primitive, holy; his features utterly compassionate. One could not but think of him as a spiritual giant.

For many years Joanna Kelley found Edward's 'total subservience to God' hard to understand. 'It seemed to me that God tested him and demanded sacrifices of him in an unreasonable, almost capricious manner. I now realize that this difficulty is one of terminology, and that what is meant is an absolute trust in an invincible power that is entirely beyond our apprehension or comprehension.' Discussing Edward's seeming unwillingness or inability to settle in a parish, a monastery, a family or any other community, Mrs Kelley declares: 'He was what might now be called a drop-out, essentially a wanderer. Yet he could not really be called a loner since he spent his life meeting people, making and keeping friends and taking an interest in them and their problems'. Perhaps, she suggests, Edward's attitude to relationships was based on his determination to have no earthly possessions. 'He did not wish to possess, and he resisted possessiveness on the part of others. His one real commitment was to God; and all other relationships, whether as son, lover, hero-worshipper, brother, friend or colleague, were to him expressions of the love of God. If he felt the least danger of any other commitment, he turned his mind to God and offered it to him in sacrifice.'

*   *   *

Village Evangelism was not fated to become one of the permanent institutions of the Church of England. It met a particular need at a particular time and then, having fulfilled its purpose, was content to retire gracefully from the scene. Although, by the date of its demise, Brother Edward, its co-founder, had been dead for fifteen years, he would almost certainly have approved the decision to wind up the VEs. He always maintained that, while the message of Christian evangelism was eternal, particular methods of passing on that message were merely ephemeral – and that therefore Village Evangelism should never allow itself to set into a mould.

The steep decline in the movement's appeal can be seen in the statistics for the missions that it undertook. Whereas, in its prime in the late 1950s, over two hundred parishes had been visited each year by teams of missioners, by 1965 the number of annual visitations had shrunk to twelve, by 1966 to six and by 1967 to four. The movement had run completely out of steam. What was the reason for VE's catastrophic collapse after its first heady decade? The answer lies partly in the changing religious climate (1963 had seen the publication of *Honest to God* and the beginning of the fashionable craze for 'religionless Christianity'); partly in the fact that, by the mid-sixties, all those parishes at all inclined to embark on a VE mission had already done so and the remainder were just not interested. Moreover (as a speaker at the valedictory conference remarked), whereas in former times most villagers had known at least *something* about Christianity, nowadays more and more people were almost totally ignorant of it – and a week of mission did not allow sufficient time first to tell them about it and then to inspire them with a desire to become Christians themselves.

This farewell conference took place at Swanwick, Derbyshire, from 27 November to 1 December 1967 under the chairmanship of Archbishop Coggan of York. About 150 people attended. Although the writing for VE was so clearly on the wall, its adherents could not, even at this eleventh hour, quite bring themselves to recognize that all was over for the movement. The final decision was therefore postponed until the following April, when a joint Anglican-Methodist conference on evangelism was being held at Keele University. By then old age and declining health had led to the retirement of Evelyn Gedge as organizer of what remained of the movement's activities; and, as no successor to her had been found, the Keele conference took the only possible decision: it deemed the role of Village Evangelism to have been fulfilled and its task ended.

On 13 May 1968 a letter breaking the news was dispatched to supporters by the movement's co-wardens, Archbishop George Appleton and Bishop George Sinker. They thanked God for the wonderful work carried out by VE over the past two decades. They recognized the need for change. They pointed out that it was necessary to die in order to live; that death always preceded life; and that supporters would still be able to infiltrate, stimulate and encourage every local effort at evangelism and the deepening of the spiritual life. Whether such truisms would have come as much comfort to the many supporters of VE who had relished the sense of fellowship engendered by parish missions may be doubted. But at least they were echoed in a letter from the Church Missionary Society which declared: 'It is a matter of great thankfulness that a movement within the Church which has been so committed to mission has had the strength and the grace to heed the direction of the Holy Spirit to close a door of the past and so to enable future doors to open'.

EPILOGUE

Readers of the foregoing pages will have been left with an impression of overpowering sanctity. Indeed some may feel that the subjects of these four mini-biographies were almost too good (in the most literal sense) to be true. If their reputation for holiness depended merely on my own estimate of their characters, then there would be some truth in this charge. But it rests not on my judgement alone but on that of countless contemporaries of the four from all sections of society. One witness might be unreliable or biased; the combined testimony of a cloud of witnesses cannot so easily be dismissed. So, when Fr Andrew is described as a radiator of holiness, or Brother Douglas as a modern St Francis, or Fr George as 'the only true Christian I have ever met', or Brother Edward as the most Christ-like man a bishop had ever known, the authors of the tributes speak (as I have shown) for a host of others. The light of my four heroes shone with such a burning intensity as to illuminate their good works for all to see.

It is an intriguing exercise to examine briefly what the four had in common. Three came from a comfortable background, their fathers being respectively an Indian Army officer, a Wesleyan minister and writer, and a farmer-turned-businessman. Only George Potter had a humble origin, his father having been a railway clerk who died when George was a baby. All four enjoyed a particularly close relationship with their mother.

Andrew, when a few days old, had shared with his the traumatic episode of the panther who came by night; Douglas, whose birth might have endangered his mother's life, confesses to having been a 'mother's boy'; George found himself having from an early age to help support his mother financially in her long widowhood; Edward, as a fourteenth child, was the fruit of a difficult pregnancy, and also of much prayer. All four responded with a loving care and affection.

In their educational backround three of the four followed a common pattern of public school (Clifton, Dulwich, Haileybury) and Oxford University. Once again George was the odd man out, opting for Kelham and King's College, London. But George's schooling locally was no barrier to his developing an early sense of vocation (at the age of nine, he tells us). Douglas too says that he had determined to be both a missionary and a Franciscan while still at school, and Edward that it was at Haileybury that he first became aware of his vocation to the ministry. Andrew, in spite of having found his confirmation a 'vital experience', appears to have gone on to Oxford without any set religious convictions. In his case it was first the crucial meeting with Winnington-Ingram and then the traumatic experience which ended at the altar in Bethnal Green that spurred him towards ordination. Edward enjoyed the parallel experience of the Albert Hall meeting and the first confession to an Oxford priest. Douglas claims to have been led to take the pledge to serve overseas as a result of his successful prayer to obtain a place in a victorious college boat.

Once the decision to be ordained was taken, however, differences of tempo appear. For Andrew there was no doubt whatever about his vocation to the religious life – he went straight from theological college to join his SDC colleagues at Plaistow and was priested in a monastic habit. Edward needed only a short curacy to be convinced that the parochial ministry was not for him. In the end the religious life in the traditional sense was not for him either, though he seemed to many a religious in all but name. In the case of both Douglas and George the path to the Franciscan way of life came after a longish spell in the parochial ministry, interrupted in both cases by chaplaincy duty during the First World War. But, though they might have started later than the other two, they soon made up lost ground; and both the Brotherhood of St Francis of Assisi and the Brotherhood of the Holy Cross rivalled the Society of the Divine Compassion in depth of prayer and multiplicity of good works. It was their genius for combining faith and works in their ministry of compassion that distinguished these Franciscan-based communities. The proportions of course varied. Sometimes the BSFA in its pre-merger days and the BHC seemed to traditionalists to sit lightly to the claims of a proper monastic discipline. To such as these the SDC seemed to have got the mixture more nearly right. But both the post-Andrew SDC and the post-George BHC soon folded after the deaths of their founding fathers: once the founder's charisma had been removed by death, recruits were impossible to find. In the case of the BSFA, as I have shown, it was the merger with the Brotherhood of the Love of Christ that saved it from the slow decline which must inevitably have overtaken it as Douglas grew old. In the event it was the ideal combination of Douglas and Algy that led to a new lease of life for their merged communities. Left to himself, Douglas would have neglected his own community for his wayfarers. The gibe that the members of the BSFA were only 'social workers in brown habits' was too near the bone to make comfortable hearing. In the same way the BHC was not most people's idea of a traditional religious community. For George the 'religious system' was always secondary to the people whom it was designed to serve; hence his refusal to toe the orthodox line where traditional observances were concerned. George was a 'loner', in that his community depended too much on one man, himself. Edward too was a 'loner', in the sense that he refused in the end to contemplate becoming a traditional 'religious' because it would have involved him in taking the vow of obedience to a fallible human being which he felt should only be offered to God himself. To Edward the vows were the crux of the matter. Even when he attempted to run a religious community of his own at Westcote it soon came to grief: partly because (like George Potter) he was too often absent, but also because he ran into the minefield of what constitutes a religious community and refused to be trammelled by the demands of even a modest amount of monastic routine. In the end he found his niche in the Village Evangelists, though he survived by only a few years the foundation of the movement which he had helped to inspire.

Edward was, however, undoubtedly cast in the Franciscan mould and might have fitted quite easily into at least the pre-merger community at Hilfield if only he could have got round that awkward obstacle of the monastic vows. So back we are at Hilfield, and the wheel has come full circle. For Hilfield still survives, and indeed grows from strength to strength. Although some may sigh for the unstructured days when Douglas reigned alone in his glory, most would agree that Hilfield needed an organizational genius like Algy to make the machine run smoothly. Both Douglas and Algy would be amazed, but no doubt delighted, at the way in which the Society of St Francis has expanded over the years. The present set-up under a Minister-General, with four provinces spread across the globe, seems light years away from the humble beginnings in the Dorset countryside. But the enlarged SSF is undoubtedly meeting the needs of the times.

The mother house at Hilfield still retains the special affections of supporters of the society; and here, each summer, tertiaries and other friends with their families assemble for a camp in the friary grounds. And, although Hilfield is now only one of over a dozen Franciscan houses in the UK, it contrives to maintain an ambitious programme of good works. It still provides short-term accommodation for unemployed and homeless wayfarers. It provides other men with sheltered accommodation on a long-term basis. Another half-dozen or so men requiring rehabilitation (often addicts or men on parole) live at the friary for a year or more, while a dozen short-stay visitors can seek spiritual refreshment and renewal in peaceful surroundings in the friary's guest-house. Each year up to a hundred educational groups visit the friary, which serves as a resource centre for schoolchildren, undergraduates and other young people. Hilfield also accommodates novices in training for membership of the SSF. Training is educational as well as vocational, and incorporates theology, social studies and counselling skills. The society's British branch houses are at Alnmouth, Birmingham, Cambridge, Glasshampton, Great Witley, Liverpool, Paddington, Plaistow, Scunthorpe, Stepney, Edinburgh, Glasgow and Belfast. The UK constitutes the society's European Province; there are in addition provinces for America, Australia/New Zealand and the Pacific Islands.

Douglas began his caring ministry to the outcasts of society in the days before the advent of the Welfare State. With the contraction of the Welfare State, and with the provision of social services falling more and more on voluntary bodies, the need for the caring ministry of the Society of St Francis becomes more and more apparent. Although many of the modern outcasts of society may seem very different from those to whom Douglas ministered so faithfully between the wars, their need is equally urgent. It is a need that is being met by the modern brown brothers in a spirit of self-sacrifice that must surely rejoice the heart of the co-founder of the SSF as a true example of the Franciscan way.

NOTES ON SOURCES

Chapter One: Fr Andrew

A great deal of material concerning the Society of the Divine Compassion can be found in the 'Society of St Francis Deposit' in the Bodleian Library at Oxford. It includes various minute-books both of the SDC Chapter and of the PCC of St Philip's, Plaistow, together with note-books filled with sermons, retreat addresses and meditations by Fr Andrew and others of the SDC brethren. Also at the Bodleian are two rare items relating to the early days of the SDC: an article by Andrew in *The Green Quarterly* (an obscure Anglo-Catholic journal) on the society's origins; and a copy of the privately published *A Franciscan Revival*, edited by A. Clifton Kelway.

Personal letters to or from Andrew are thin on the ground at the Bodleian, though there are probably a fair number remaining in private hands. Andrew was a voluminous correspondent, and his numerous letters of spiritual counsel would no doubt have been treasured by the recipients. Kathleen E. Burne's *The Life and Letters of Father Andrew* remains the only full-length biography. T.P. Stevens's *Father Adderley* and Geoffrey Curtis's *William of Glasshampton* contain useful material on the society's early and middle period.

Chapter Two: Brother Douglas

In a letter he wrote to Douglas in December 1956, less than a year before his death, George Seaver warned: 'I am sorry for your sake that you will not be allowed to escape without a "Life" of you being written, but it is one of the penalties one has to pay for trying to "be good" – as you have tried all your life and have succeeded'. Douglas took the hint and, during his final illness, compiled a 'log-book' of reminiscences for the benefit of posterity. The log-book was 'affectionately inscribed' to Coleman Jennings, according to whom it opened with a characteristic Douglas touch: 'In case an attempt may be made on my "life" after I am gone, I leave a few notes which may perhaps stay the hand of the assassin when he finds out a little more about me'.

The log-book itself has vanished – in the sense that I was unable to track it down either in the archives room at Hilfield or at the Bodleian in Oxford. The probability is that it passed into the hands of Jennings and remains in the possession of his family. But it must obviously have been used by Fr Francis, SSF (William Tyndale-Biscoe), to form the basis of his biography of Brother Douglas, which appeared in 1959. At the beginning of his book he acknowledges his debt to Douglas, 'who spent many hours during his last painful illness recounting his stories, with the result that many of them are verbatim from his own lips and attest the facts of his life'. In the case of anyone of lesser integrity than Douglas a cynic might retort that he would have presented the facts as he wished them to appear rather than as they necessarily were. In Douglas's case no such imputation could conceivably be made – though of course it is possible that, after the lapse of time, his memory may occasionally have let him down.

A year after the appearance of Fr Francis's life a second book about Douglas was published. This was *Tales of Brother Douglas*, the first part of which was by George Seaver and the second part by Coleman Jennings. Seaver's links with Douglas went back to the 1920s; Jennings entered his life a decade later, but became in the course of time his 'dearest friend of all'. Seaver was already a writer of distinction, with much-acclaimed lives of Albert Schweitzer and Edward Wilson of the Antarctic to his credit. Jennings had written to him in 1951 to suggest that he produce a book on Douglas ('perhaps a biography is not just what I have in mind, but rather the portrait of a man who glides in and out of the picture'). In the event nothing happened immediately; but the 'portrait' appeared eventually in 1960 as an anecdotal but fascinating account of Douglas's ministry – and as a joint tribute from the pens of Seaver and Jennings.

The archives of the Society of St Francis are divided between Hilfield and the Bodleian and include a fair number of letters to and from Douglas. No.38 of the SSF journal, *The Franciscan*, which appeared in the autumn of 1957, is devoted entirely to Douglas; it includes the texts of the panegyrics preached at the two solemn requiems, together with accounts of the various facets of his ministry by friends who had known him well. The Hilfield archives also include the text of a broadcast, *Brother Douglas: Apostle of the Outcast*, written and compiled by Denis Constanduros and transmitted on the BBC Home Service on 2 April 1960. The programme told the story of his life largely through the recorded voices of people in many walks of life who remembered him.

Chapter Three: Fr George

Historical material concerning the Brotherhood of the Holy Cross is thin on the ground. According to the late Fr Francis, George Potter's successor as Father-Guardian, the BHC records were destroyed by the late Fr Giles when he joined the SSF in 1963. Francis made this disclosure to Brother John Charles, SSF, when he was interviewed on 26 June 1971, but suggested no reason why Giles should have acted as he did. Whatever his motives, the 'SSF Deposit' at the Bodleian Library in Oxford, which nominally includes the BHC archives, contains singularly little material relating to the Brotherhood – except for Brother John Charles's transcripts of his various interviews, and for an incomplete file of the *BHC Quarterly*.

I have come across few letters to or from Fr Potter; and the prime source for my narrative has therefore had to be his two autobiographical volumes, *Father Potter of Peckham* (1955) and *More Father Potter of Peckham* (1958), in which of course allowance has to be made for the subjectivity of the author. The other prime source of material is the *BHC Quarterly*, which keeps track of the Brotherhood's various twists and turns during its forty-year life.

Chapter Four: Brother Edward

At the time that I was writing this book a great deal of material relating both to Brother Edward himself and to the Village Evangelists was stored in the London home of Mrs Joanna Kelley, who had inherited it from Evelyn Gedge and who kindly allowed me to go through it. It includes many letters *from* Brother Edward (though very few *to* him). Mrs Kelley was hoping, at the time of my visit, to hand on all this material to some national Church society or organization for safe keeping. She herself has compiled a biographical memoir of Brother Edward, *The White Hyacinth* (so far unpublished), which forms a valuable supplement to Kenneth Packard's 'official' life and which takes the story up to the demise of the Village Evangelist movement in 1968.

BIBLIOGRAPHY

Andrew, Father, SDC (H.E. Hardy), *The Adventure of Faith*. Mowbray 1933.

Anson, Peter F., *The Call of the Cloister*. SPCK, 4th edition, 1964.

Bull, Norman J., *A Modern Saint Francis: The Story of Brother Douglas*. Religious and Moral Education Press 1983.

Burne, Kathleen E., *The Life and Letters of Father Andrew*, SDC. Mowbray 1948.

Carey, Walter, *Good-Bye to my Generation*. Mowbray 1951.

Curtis, Geoffrey, CR, *William of Glasshampton: Friar, Monk, Solitary*. SPCK 1947.

Denis, Father, SSF (D.W. Marsh), *Father Algy*. Hodder & Stoughton 1964

Duggan, Margaret, *The Convent of the Sisters of the Community of Jesus of Nazareth, Westcote*. Westcote Local History Society 1993

Edward, Brother (E.G. Bulstrode), ed., *Behold, Thy King Cometh!* Canterbury Press 1950.

Fisher, Michael (R.L.), SSF, *For the Time Being: A Memoir*. Gracewing 1993.

Fox, John Roger, *Bridging the Gulf*. Amate Press, Oxford, 1983.

Francis, Father, SSF (W.F. Tyndale-Biscoe), *Brother Douglas: Apostle of the Outcast*. Mowbray 1959.

Kelley, Joanna, *The White Hyacinth*. Completed in 1978 but not published.

Kelway, A. Clifton, ed., *A Franciscan Revival: The Story of the Society of the Divine Compassion*. Whitwell Press, Plaistow, 1908.

Kenneth, Brother, SSF (K. Hunt), *A Brother's Way: Memoirs*. Society of St Francis 1991.

Leslie, Shane, *The Film of Memory*. Michael Joseph 1938.

Packard, Kenneth, *Brother Edward: Priest and Evangelist*. Geoffrey Bles 1955.

Parsons, Stephen, *The Challenge of Christian Healing*. SPCK 1986

Paul, Elizabeth, *A Faithful Witness. An Anthology of Brother Edward's Teaching*. Hodder & Stoughton 1966.

Potter, George, *Father Potter of Peckham: A South London Saga*. Hodder & Stoughton 1955.

Potter, George, *More Father Potter of Peckham*. Hodder & Stoughton 1958.

Seaver, George, and Jennings, Coleman, *Tales of Brother Douglas*. Mowbray 1960.

Stevens, T.P., *Father Adderley*. T. Werner Laurie 1943.

Williams, Barrie, *The Franciscan Revival in the Anglican Communion*. Darton, Longman & Todd 1982.

INDEX